I GOT THE FISH IN THE HEAD

A RADIATORS RETROSPECTIVE

By
Jay Mazza

FORWARD BY REGGIE SCANLAN OF THE RADIATORS

ISBN: 1456483293
ISBN-13: 9781456483296

For Ann—she's not a fishhead, but she loves one!

Acknowledgements

I would like to thank the members of the Radiators, their intrepid soundman Kenny Samuels, their manager Josh Abelson as well as members of the crew past and present for thirty-three years of amazing music and good times. I would also like to thank all of the individuals and companies that helped spread fishhead music. Thanks are also due to various record company executives and agents who graciously hired me to write about my favorite band and the many editors who indulged or encouraged my work.

Special thanks to Tony Martin, Mike Williamson, Reggie Scanlan, Rob Rudner, James "Dylan" Stansbury, Tony Zucker, Paul Toracinta, Karl Bremer, Chris Weddle, Renette Dejoie-Hall, Steve Novak, Tom Speed, Barney Kilpatrick, "Baton Rouge" Bill Boelens, Kingsley Stoken, Glenn "Kul" Sears, Sandy Horowitz, Andy Ambrose, Yakir Katz, Paul Bel, Wesley J. Schmidt and the dancing girls.

This book is dedicated to my parents, Dotty and Jack Mazza — with appreciation and gratitude

Cover art by Mike Williamson

Foreword

Ever since stepping off the boat in the Crescent City (ostensibly to attend college), Jay Mazza has been absorbing, celebrating and writing about the music and musicians of New Orleans. Years of marching in second-line parades, hangin' out in dressing rooms 'til five in the morning and attending more musical performances than can be counted have given him the knowledge and experience to write about the scene. It also has allowed him to form the friendships and make the contacts that allow a degree of intimacy with his subjects that is rare. But access and opportunity are only part of the equation. The other part is the ability to write objectively about what is being experienced. That is what makes his writings so relevant. Always entertaining and witty, they ultimately seek to educate, which is one of the strengths of his work.

My first memory of Jay dates back to the days when I was performing in the Radiators at Luigi's Pizza Parlor, thirty years ago. He was a just-got-to-town joker I would see at the gigs. Eventually we started talking and getting to know each other. It was the beginning of a cool and valued friendship. His knowledge of the local music scene was, and remains, encyclopedic. When I come off the road and need to know what's happening in the clubs, Jay is the first and only call.

—Reggie Scanlan
Bassist for the Radiators

Preface

On November 7, 2010, my phone rang in the middle of a critical game during the Saints follow-up season as Super Bowl champions. Thinking something serious must have happened for someone to call during the game, I glanced at the caller ID and saw that it was Reggie Scanlan, the bassist for the Radiators. He was at the St. Louis airport and wanted to deliver some news before I started hearing rumors. Shortly after, another call came in from Dave Malone, the band's singer and guitarist. The news was shocking. The band was breaking up.

Reggie briefly relayed the facts. Ed Volker, the principal songwriter, keyboardist and leader of the group for thirty-three years, was tired of traveling. He informed his bandmates that he was finished fighting the rigors of the road. He intended to honor all of their commitments, which I understood to mean their longstanding traditional closing slot at the New Orleans Jazz and Heritage Festival in early May.

Two months later, the shock has not worn off. I have seen the Radiators perform hundreds of times over the past thirty-two years since I was seventeen years old. Many of the milestones in my life have been celebrated in their company. I met many of my dearest friends while grooving to the band. I have traveled from coast to coast and even across the Atlantic Ocean to experience the pleasures of their music. A story I wrote about the European tour in 2001 closes these pages.

I never saw it coming. The five original members have stayed together through ups and downs that would have destroyed most other groups. They have weathered the travails of the music business and emerged intact while the industry is in tatters. The career of the Radiators has spanned every recording medium—their first recording was a 45-RPM single that was released in 1978—from vinyl through cassettes, digital audio tapes, CDs and now digital downloads. But most importantly, their music has matured like the proverbial fine wine. They sound better than ever as a band—that's saying a lot considering they have played over 4400 shows. I assumed it wouldn't be over until it was really over.

When I first saw the Radiators perform, I was neither familiar with their original music, even as it moved me deeply, nor did I know much of the music that inspired them. I learned about New Orleans R&B, 1960s-era rock, soul, the blues, and country music on dance floors across New Orleans while I was in college. I also learned how complementary musicians interacting can create a sound that is so much bigger than the sum of its parts.

Though I didn't know it at the time, this musical education was preparing me for my life's work. It was ten years after first hearing the Radiators perform that I decided to become a writer focused on the unique music and culture of New Orleans. The first couple of pieces that I had published were about the band. They are contained within these pages.

A RADIATORS RETROSPECTIVE

In order to help remember performances that I attended and to better inform my writing, I began keeping a music journal in April of 1989. There are hundreds of entries about performances by members of the Radiators, but one sticks out. During Jazz Fest in April of 2001, Ed Volker's side project, Zeke Fishhead's Jolly House, was the backing band for the legendary New Orleans R&B singer/songwriter/guitarist Earl King. This is what I wrote in my journal about that performance: "They are on fire from the get-go. Earl comes out halfway through the first set and rips. It is very psychedelic and he is in fine form. After the break, the band does one tune, 'Junco Partner,' and then Earl unexpectedly does the rest of the set. They have to repeat 3 songs, but it's still great even though it lags at the end. Earl only stumbles once and knocks over his mic stand while playing behind his head. Zeke plays maracas almost the whole second set."

I went on to write more about the Radiators, examples from other publications are also collected here, but I also began exploring the music and the musicians who inspired them. For thirteen years I was the music writer for the Louisiana Weekly—one of the oldest African-American newspapers in the country. I was the white boy at the black paper covering the music that I loved.

I also started a publicity company and began writing press releases and bios. The Radiators were one of my first clients. Those efforts are here as well.

I began working on my first large-scale project—a book that examines the era of New Orleans that helped me find myself. It is part history and part memoir and looks back at the music and culture of the last quarter of the twentieth century. An excerpt about the Radiators begins this book.

Since that fateful day in November 2010, I have worked on "I Got the Fish in the Head." It is neither comprehensive nor complete. It is not comprehensive because I felt compelled to produce the first volume within the same deadline as the band. It is not complete because as of this writing, no one knows what will become of the Radiators. Their music will live on forever—nearly every show has been taped since the mid-1980s. Like the Grateful Dead before them, the Radiators are likely to generate new fans as each generation discovers the depth and breadth of their music. But most importantly, each of the members of the band will continue to make music—at this point in their lives to go silent would be impossible. But the future of the quintet beyond the last show on June 11, 2011 is uncertain.

1/11/11

I Got the Fish in the Head

This piece is an excerpt from the original draft of "Up Front and Center—New Orleans Music at the End of the Twentieth Century." Publication of the full book is pending.

The first band I actually remember seeing in New Orleans was the Cartoons. The show was at the Maple Leaf in the fall of 1979. The Cartoons featured two musicians who went on to have successful careers in the music business and one who died a premature death and is remembered as a seminal figure on the scene.

Becky Kury was the bassist and one of the vocalists. Before her stint in the Cartoons she was a member of the Rhapsodizers, a fondly remembered group of New Orleans R&B fanatics that also featured future members of the Radiators—the keyboardist, vocalist, and songwriter Ed Volker, the guitarist Camile Boudoin, and the drummer Frank Bua. Kury died young and for years the wall on the Broadway side of the K&B drug store (now a Rite Aid) at the corner of St. Charles Avenue sported the semi-cryptic message, "Becky Kury Lives." Every time it was painted over, which was often, the phrase reappeared overnight clearly vexing the building's owners.

Kury was essentially the front woman of the Cartoons and her vocals were soulful and warm. She could wail like the proverbial banshee, but she also projected a vulnerability that endeared her to other musicians and to the male members of the audience.

Tommy Malone, then barely in his twenties, was the guitarist for the Cartoons, and he also sang. He is now a member of the subdudes and a well-respected musician nationally. Even at such a young age, Malone was already showing the prodigious technique that has served him well throughout his long career. His playing had hints of the blues, but with a clear, precise tone that was jazzier than that of most of his peers.

Kenny Blevins was the drummer, and he was a time-keeping monster. His cymbal accents were impeccable and his playing was firmly rooted in the drum tradition of New Orleans. In his career after the Cartoons, Blevins has played and recorded with many important Louisiana acts such as Sonny Landreth, John Mooney, George Porter Jr., Earl King, Zachary Richard, and Michael Doucet of Beausoleil as well as roots rock star John Hiatt. He relocated to Nashville some years back, and he currently works as a studio musician.

The Cartoons were a band that I immediately found interesting because they mined the fertile territory of New Orleans R&B and performed some of the songs that I loved from listening to the Rolling Stones. However, as a Tulane freshman, I was still not aware of the deep connections between my high school fascination with the Stones and the music of New Orleans. That came later as I developed an understanding of the history of American music.

While I enjoyed the music of the Cartoons, I intuitively knew that there was something missing, and that something, I discovered after hearing the Radiators for the first time, was original music. The Radiators also played at the Maple Leaf, and their concerts back in the day were epic, three-set affairs that usually didn't end until four a.m. However, it wasn't an original song that first caused me to become smitten by the Radiators. It was a Rolling Stones song.

The Stones were not the first of many bands that I fixated on, though they are the only band of my high school years to whom I still feel an allegiance. That honor goes to Aerosmith—a band I saw four times before moving to New Orleans. But once I heard the Rolling Stones, I realized that Aerosmith was just an American imitation of those edgy British rockers. Like many other suburban kids in the 1970s, I knew absolutely nothing at all about the great blues and R&B artists that constituted the well that the Stones had been drinking from since the early 1960s.

The song was "Dead Flowers." The chorus, which fans of both groups love to sing lustily, ends with the words, "and I won't forget to put roses on your grave." What made the Radiators version of the song so compelling was the way they syncopated the melody of that line, adding a swinging lilt to it that completely transformed the song while actually stretching it out.

I GOT THE FISH IN THE HEAD

It wasn't just the musical transformation of the song that hit me hard. It was also the way that Ed Volker sings the line and then adds his own qualifier, "...big ole long stem roses," which shook me to my very core. How was it possible that this group of young musicians from New Orleans could improve on a tune by the world's greatest rock 'n' roll band?

But improve it they did. What I didn't know at the time, but came to understand intimately, was how that seemingly slight musical shift falls directly within the parameters of the New Orleans groove. They didn't change the song to make it better, that would have been asking a bit too much, but they adjusted it to make it their own and in doing so they turned it into a New Orleans song.

Needless to say, I was hooked. Over the course of the next thirty-plus years, I have seen the Radiators play hundreds of shows. I became obsessed in a way I had never been before, and I loved it. They moved me and aroused a new passion for music that was always a part of my spirit.

I routinely chose to see the Radiators over bigger, better-known acts that were usually playing at Tipitina's. I started traveling to see them play on the North Shore. Saturday nights at the Dream Palace on Frenchmen Street, a long journey in more ways than one from my place uptown, eventually became a required destination.

By the beginning of my sophomore year, I found out about Luigi's, a pizza place on Elysian Fields Avenue near the Lakefront that was home to a whole different cast of characters since it was close to the University of New Orleans, a school with a much higher percentage of locals than Tulane. The front of the bar had booths befitting a college hangout. But I don't think I ever walked into the front door, preferring to enter on the side where the band was set up.

If I thought getting to the Faubourg Marigny on a Saturday night was tough, it was nothing compared to getting to the Lakefront on Wednesday night. But Luigi's was free and though the Radiators' cover charge during that time period was only two dollars (one dollar at the Maple Leaf!), it was a lot of money. Boiled crawfish were fifty-nine cents a pound and a six-pack of Dixie was under three dollars.

I recall numerous Wednesday nights heading to "Highball Night" at the Boot, the closest bar to Tulane and longtime hangout for the hippie contingent of students. Back then Tulane was much more firmly divided into two camps. The aforementioned hippies generally eschewed the fraternity crowd, with the exception of Phi Kappa Sigma, the so-called "music frat." The frat crowd hung out one block toward the river on Broadway at Tin Lizzy's. No one I hung out with went to Tin Lizzy's, and no one who went to Tin Lizzy's would be caught at the Boot.

"Highball Night" was a big attraction, since the bar sold mixed drinks for fifty cents. There was always a gigantic crowd in various states of inebriation, and I would go in the hopes of finding someone who wanted to drive out to the lake to see the Radiators. Needless to say, I didn't always succeed in the pursuit of a sober driver or someone who would trust me to drive if they were already intoxicated. However, virtually every person that I coerced or convinced to make the drive became hardcore fans, who were dubbed "fishheads" after the band started describing their sound to writers as "fish-head music."

On Wednesday nights, they would move some of the tables out of the way, and the band would set up in a back corner by the bathrooms. To get to the ladies room, the women had to walk by the side of the stage, past Volker's keyboard and percussion rig. The ceiling was impossibly low, adorned with cheap wooden chandeliers that dangled precariously. It was a simple set up. There was no formal dance floor and when it got crowded, which happened shortly after the Radiators started getting a modicum of notice in the local press, the crowd was right up in the musicians' faces. The space was so tight that the drums, which weren't even on a riser, were nearly at the front of the band.

For the Radiators, Luigi's was like a weekly rehearsal session. The crowd was mostly friends of the band and UNO students. They would play three sets working out new material and throwing caution to the wind with respect to a conventional performance. Part of the thrill also had to do with the crazy clientele who populated the bar and were immortalized years later in Volker's song, "The Wrong Road." There was "Too Tall" Tim, the bartender, a longhaired blonde in tight jeans that embodied the Roger Daltrey look. He always had a crowd of young women around until the band hit. Then the women gravitated like spawning salmon to the dance floor.

Another bartender, Ramon, played a major part in one of the most insane episodes that ever occurred at Luigi's. After the gig was over he tells the band that he's going to make everyone a flaming drink. Despite the fact that he has already consumed more than enough, he lines up the glasses, including one for Too Tall Tim and one for himself. As he begins pouring the booze, it's clear that most of the alcohol is landing on the bar and all over his hands. He proceeds to light the drinks anyway and in an instant the whole bar is covered in flames. Ramon's hands are actually on fire, but he's so intoxicated that he starts patting his face with his flaming hands. Luckily Tim was quick enough to get some wet bar towels, otherwise serious injury was likely. But for thirty seconds or so, mayhem was the operative word.

The place even had a legendary character, "Willie Burn Your Shirt," who I only had the privilege of seeing in action a single time. His shtick was insane. His favorite song was an instrumental, "Texas Chainsaw Massacre," which the band wrote after seeing the iconic horror film. When they began playing the long intro to the song, Willie would perform a redneck striptease. After he removed his shirt, he would pull out a lighter and ignite it. Since the popular shirts of the day were 100 percent polyester, the garment instantly caught fire and began a slow, noxious burn. Then he would swing the burning garment over his head simultaneous amusing and scaring the wits out of the rest of the patrons and the band.

Given the free-for-all nature of Luigi's, even some of the Tulane students who started gravitating to the bar on Wednesday nights got caught up in the intensity. One night right before graduation in 1982, an infamous frat boy showed up already drunk with a half yard in his hands. He managed to get through the dancers up front while swinging the eighteen-inch tall, thin glass container dangerously close to

Dave Malone's microphone stand. If he had shattered the glass directly in front of the band, a quart of spilled beer would have been the least of his problems. Gary Phillips, the gigantic roadie who worked with the Radiators throughout their early years, was watching him closely and had already warned him several times to stay away from the gear.

Gary was a genuinely good-hearted fellow as long as no one messed with the band. In one notorious episode at the MOMs Ball, an underground Mardi Gras party that the Radiators have performed at during every year of their existence, he punched the king of the krewe backstage at the ball. Gary didn't realize at the time that the drunk was actually royalty–he was just doing his job as security for the band. To add to the king's embarrassment at causing a disturbance in the band's private area was the fact that Gary was in drag at the time. The king commented when he woke up on the floor, "Man, that dyke sure can throw a punch!"

Seeing the Radiators, especially the midweek shows at Luigi's, was like an intensive musical education. I learned about many different artists, and I was exposed to many new genres of music listening to the Radiators. They covered such a wide range of tunes that each night I heard dozens of new songs, including many classic New Orleans R&B songs, from Eddie Bo to Professor Longhair, which was the wellspring of their sound, as well as songs from rock 'n' roll, the blues, country, soul music, and so much more.

I was still very naïve musically. I didn't know much about the development of American music, but by the time I was a full-fledged fishhead I had learned a lot more than any course or series of books could have taught me. Since the Radiators played so many styles, I ended up absorbing so much music that I credit them with being responsible for a big part of my musical education.

Going to see the Radiators was like listening to a radio station that had room for everybody from Robert Johnson to Credence Clearwater Revival, from Bo Diddley to Johnny Cash. But there were also moments that were embarrassing in retrospect. After seeing them a dozen or so times, I began to recognize many of the songs that the Radiators covered, but I usually didn't know who wrote them until much later. But since Ed Volker was a prolific songwriter, new original songs were always popping into the mix. In my early days as a fan, I usually didn't know whether a song I had never heard before was a new one from the pen of Volker or whether it was a cover with which I was unfamiliar. I actually thought Clarence Carter's "Slip Away" was an original tune for so long that it was simply too ridiculous to even discuss when I found out its true provenance.

Of course in retrospect, that confusion was actually a sign of a band and a songwriter that had something special going on. If Volker's original songs could vie with a classic like "Slip Away," then they must have been a good band even as young musicians.

The Radiators had a part-time percussionist and vocalist, Glen "Kul" Sears, who was heavily into the Grateful Dead, and he brought some of that influence to the band. While Sears was known to sing the occasional Dead song and also fronted a Grateful Dead cover band called Remedy at the time, he was more likely to be called up during a Radiators show for a cover tune like "Turn On Your Lovelight," which was in both bands' repertoire. Their loose style of playing had a lot in common with the Grateful Dead's opened-ended approach to live music. Both bands shared the same sentiment about instrumental solos, and they loved to jam.

But during this period, before the advent of "jam bands," this loose-limbed, fly-by-the-seat-of-your-pants style of playing was uncommon in popular music, and many Deadheads in New Orleans gravitated to the Radiators because of the similarities in their approach to the music. The Radiators and the Grateful Dead also shared the same attitude about taping their shows. Both bands encouraged taping, and tapers at Radiators shows were common by the early 1980s.

The Grateful Dead and the Radiators shared other musical characteristics that separated them from other bands, which were popular at the time. They didn't usually play with set lists, letting the crowd and the vibe determine the next song. They also liked to segue from one song into another, creating an unbroken chain of music. With both bands, this could go on for the length of a set.

But more significant was the fact that that both bands shared a similar affection for what is now called Americana music. Both groups were fascinated by the role of country music and the blues in the developing style of rock 'n' roll. They both played cover songs that explored the connection between the various styles.

During the early 1980s, the Grateful Dead were touring prolifically, but they had not returned to New Orleans in over ten years following the infamous drug arrest in 1970 that inspired the line, "busted down on Bourbon Street" in the song "Truckin'." So when school began in the fall of 1980, the Deadheads in my peer group at Tulane were all atwitter. The Grateful Dead were finally returning to New Orleans for a two-night stand at the Saenger Theater on Canal Street. Excitement was high because the two gigs were also part of a now-legendary run of three-set shows that began in San Francisco and culminated with an unprecedented twelve nights at Radio City Music Hall in New York City. The Grateful Dead planned to play the first set each night acoustically. New Orleans was the only other city being treated to such a musical extravaganza, and my friends were hyped beyond belief.

In order to secure the best seats, we hatched a plan to stay up all night in front of the Ticketmaster office to be the first in line when the tickets went on sale. Conveniently, the office was on Tulane's campus, a stone's throw from Phelps Hall, where I lived during freshman year. We arrived in the late afternoon prepared to work shifts all night long. My friends and I were not the only ones with the same idea, and by nightfall there was a decent-sized crowd prepared to wait all night. Some enterprising fellow removed a couch from one of the dorm's lounges and the scene was set for an all night party.

Amazingly, Tulane's campus police—known as "Greenies" after one of Tulane's colors—didn't try to control the line or the crowd. We simply policed ourselves, and I remember the night as being an epic evening of laughter, music (of course, exclusively the music of the Dead) and conspiratorial camaraderie.

The night of the first show, my two roommates and I took the streetcar from our place on Dante Street to Canal Street.

I GOT THE FISH IN THE HEAD

The scene outside the Saenger looked exactly like the one outside of Nassau Coliseum in Long Island, where I had seen the Grateful Dead for the first time earlier in the year. It appeared that the sixties were still in full bloom, as the shows seemed to have attracted every hippie and neo-hippie within hundreds of miles.

Inside the theater, the staff tried in vain to control the crowd, to keep them in their seats and out of the aisles. I had not been to the Saenger before and was immediately taken by the building—now here's a place to have a concert! It was so different than the gigantic rooms that I was used to for big shows. The statuary surrounding the floor level orchestra seating and the incredible ceiling that looked like the night sky complete with twinkling stars created the effect of being in an ancient Roman amphitheatre.

Of course, due to our diligence in acquiring tickets, we had great seats—within the first ten rows—for both nights. The band sounded great. It was so much more intimate than hearing them in a giant facility designed for professional sports. The acoustic sets were incredible. The Grateful Dead's music, while differentiated by long winding jams and interesting segues between songs, was rooted in Americana. All of their folk and country influences came to the forefront when they played acoustically.

Like my new favorite band in New Orleans, the Radiators, they didn't repeat one song over the two nights. There was no obvious difference in quality between the two shows as there was earlier in the year on Long Island. While I knew numerous people who went up to New York to see them play at Radio City,

16

four shows inside of six months was plenty for me although I eventually went on to see the Grateful Dead perform another fifteen times before they disbanded in 1995 following the death of lead guitarist Jerry Garcia.

Years after those first performances, the Dead released a live recording called *Live Without a Net*. That album title summed up everything that was attractive to me about the music of the Grateful Dead. They went on stage without a set list and just let the music take them, and the crowd, without much regard to where they were going. Sure, there were set patterns that could be anticipated by the Deadheads, such as certain songs almost always being played at certain times and tunes that always seg-ued together. But in essence, the music of the Grateful Dead, at least how they performed it live, can be explained with the popular aphorism, "it's about the journey, not the destination."

In certain ways, my early fascination with the Grateful Dead was reflected years later as I developed a serious affin-ity for jazz. The Dead were all about improvisation, both indi-vidually and collectively. As in jazz, each member got his turn soloing and some of the more compelling moments that oc-curred within each performance came about through collec-tive improvisation.

While no one would call the Grateful Dead a jazz band, over the years they attracted a fair number of jazz musicians who jammed with them. Prominent among them was Branford Marsalis, the eldest son of the famous New Orleans jazz family. He took a large measure of grief from his younger and stri-dently anti-pop brother Wynton as well as the jazz establish-ment for playing with "that hippie band."

But Marsalis recognized that the music of Dead was not about how many key changes or chords there are in a given song. It was not about how many tricky shifts in meter occurred, nor was it about any of the conventional ways that music is categorized. He knew that the members of the band, particularly Garcia on lead guitar and Phil Lesh on electric bass, were masterful improvisers.

Communication between the members of a band that focuses on improvisation is the most important factor in producing a top-notch performance. Within the Grateful Dead and within most working jazz bands, that communication often borders on the telepathic. Each musician is aware of what is happening as it happens, and they usually can anticipate what is going to come next in a particular musical framework.

As in jazz, that was the attraction for Marsalis and that was the attraction for me. The feeling that this could go anywhere musically and the idea that the music is not constrained by structure was paramount.

The give-and-take as the energy flows between the audience and the musicians (and among the musicians themselves) is most easily understood by concentrating on the sound itself and training the ear to hear the subtleties within the music. In order to really appreciate jazz, the listener has to pay close attention to the intricacies of the music each individual is producing as well as the collective efforts of the group. Otherwise all that is heard is a generalized sound—a vague sense of tempo and rhythm amid an instrumental wash.

The same can be said for the music of the Grateful Dead. To truly enjoy a performance by the Dead, the listener has to stay focused and engaged. In essence, they have to try to become part of the band. Perhaps that is why they attracted so many fans that used psychedelic drugs to enhance the experience.

Another area of connection between the Grateful Dead and jazz concerns the role of the song. For the Dead and for most jazz musicians, the song is merely a vehicle that is used to achieve a certain level of musical expression. The song becomes the framework around which the musicians express themselves collectively. But for the concept to work effectively, the framework cannot constrain them as they make individual statements through soloing.

Jazz has it standards drawn from a deep well that includes songs from other eras; great compositions from the pens of jazz's greats and songs from genres such as Tin Pan Alley, the Great American Songbook, and Broadway show tunes. Within jazz, there is no stigma attached to playing standards. Standards are the common language that allows jazz musicians to be instantly on the same page with each other.

Within pop music, the relationship between original songs and covers plays out differently. For a pop band to be great they have to write their own music, and a band that plays only covers is usually looked down on and denigrated as "just a cover band." The Grateful Dead were able to avoid that stigma because of the way that made each "cover" song their own. They also drew from a deep well of songs in a variety of American genres. Whether they were playing the blues standard "Turn On Your Lovelight," the Johnny Cash classic "Big River," or any other cover in their vast repertoire, each song functioned like a jazz standard. They were merely vehicles for improvisatory expression.

I GOT THE FISH IN THE HEAD

This is the reason that the Radiators were often compared to the Grateful Dead in their earlier days. In lesser hands "Dead Flowers" is just another Rolling Stones cover. But by making it their own, they create something new and different. The same goes for the hundreds of other songs that they cover. The songs also play the same role by providing a framework for improvisation.

After seeing the Dead up front in the intimate setting of the Saenger Theater, I began seeking that same vibe and found it in the music of Radiators. From the fall of 1980 through the spring of 1981, I went to virtually every Radiators show. They were playing at least three shows a week and I made brief notations about each performance on their newsletter, "The Fish Headlines," which I hung religiously on the front of my refrigerator every month. In the bathroom that I shared with a roommate, I had a typed note with my two favorite quotations at the time: Frederick Nietzsche's "without music, life would be a mistake," and Ed Volker's "your only limitation is your imagination."

I was sick during my first Carnival in 1980, having caught the flu when one of New Orleans' signature winter cold fronts passed through on the Saturday before Mardi Gras, leaving me drenched while dressed in shorts and a t-shirt as the temperature plunged from the mid 70s to the low 40s. So I was incredibly pumped when Carnival rolled around in 1981.

At a show about a week before the big day, Dave Malone invited me to what he described as the craziest party ever. He said it was called the MOMs ball, and the band was playing. When I pressed him for details, he said it was "out in the sticks," and it was free as long as you wore a costume. But I had noticed that

A RADIATORS RETROSPECTIVE

Dave had an obvious attraction to the girl I was hanging out with, and given my stature as a skinny twenty-year-old and his as the only rock star I knew personally, we made other plans.

Monday night, the evening before Mardi Gras, was spent in the company of a group of friends and the music of the Radiators at the Dream Palace on Frenchmen Street. The band hit the stage at their usual 11:11 p.m., and dawn was breaking over the Faubourg Marigny when the music ended. It took us a minute to realize it's Mardi Gras morning! The air was still and the thousands of revelers who would pack the streets in a few short hours were still sleeping as the unwashed night owls of the Dream Palace escaped the smoky confines of the club for the sunshine-filled dawn. We walked into the still-cool morning air and headed into the heart of the French Quarter.

With the streets basically to ourselves, we gravitated to the center of Jackson Square. The sidewalk in front of the Presbytere, on the downriver side of St. Louis Cathedral, was covered in a giant multi-colored chalk drawing. At the center of this strangely compelling abstract work of art was written in huge flowing letters, "One Size Fits All."

There were hippies with chalk, and they invited our group of young neo-hippies to add something creative to what was obviously a piece of art made collectively by the freaks. After a few added swirls we made our way into the Quarter. I didn't find out until a couple of years later that "One Size Fits All" was the theme for the MOMs Ball in 1981.

After spending the better part of the day wandering the streets of the French Quarter, my energy was flagging. We re-traced our steps and when we crossed Jackson Square, all traces of the chalk mural had been eradicated by countless numbers of painted shoes. We returned to the Dream Palace and ate our first meal in nearly 24 hours on the balcony overlooking Frenchmen Street. The restaurant was called the Reality Café.

After eating, I was wiped out like I had never been wiped out before. I got home in the early evening and slept straight through the night and half of the following day. It took me weeks to physically recover from my first proper Mardi Gras. These lyrics from The Radiators' song "Life on Mars" perfectly sum up that heady day and a half: "We came here grinning ear to ear to paint Canal Street red—it painted us instead."

In the summer of 1981, Ed Volker began playing a series of solo gigs listed as his alter ego, Zeke Fishhead. The June issue of Wavelength magazine highlighted his gig at Tipitina's with these words: "rarely does Zeke play solo." Despite that pronouncement, Volker played solo at least once a month over the course of the summer and into the fall. In Wavelength's 1983 band guide, the repertoire of his solo act was described as, "From ancient songs to the stuff I wrote this afternoon."

I went to as many of these shows as I could because I enjoyed his songs in the stripped down fashion of a solo piano gig. However, Volker didn't always play his own music. Sometimes he did all cover songs, and I remember two nights in particular when he hit the bandstand armed with a songbook. He played all Bob Dylan songs on one night, and on the other all the tunes he played were from the Grateful Dead.

Volker also configured bands featuring some of the members of the Radiators with other like-minded players. These groups were musical free-for-alls and were given whimsical monikers like Bwana Dik and the Headhunters, or Waldo and the Peppers (clearly named for the Robert Redford aviator film, "The Great Waldo Pepper," which had been a box office hit at the time). Another group featured the Radiators' guitarist and singer, Dave Malone, with his brother Tommy on guitar and his wife Suzie on vocals backed by the Radiators' rhythm section. This band was called simply, the Malones.

Volker also formed a trio along with the bassist Reggie Scanlan and the band's erstwhile percussionist and guest vocalist Glen "Kul" Sears in 1981 (Sears would become an official member of the Radiators later in 1982). The group was called Blind, Crippled and Crazy, after the O. V. Wright gutbucket classic.

Blind, Crippled and Crazy stripped the Radiators' sound down to its core. Scanlan played an upright acoustic bass, Volker had a basic keyboard set up, and Sears arrived with a set of congas. The songs they played mined the same roots as the tunes in the Radiators' repertoire, but the band delved deeper into the blues. Sears sang a few songs each set, but Volker dominated the shows. Their music was described in the 1983 band guide in Wavelength Magazine as "raggy, acoustic music about prison, wimmen, drink, railroads." That about sums it up.

Much of my experience up to that point listening to the blues was with bands led by guitarists. So I discovered many of the great blues pianists, especially the New Orleans expatriate "Champion" Jack Dupree. I also learned a whole slew of new songs from going to see Blind, Crippled and Crazy.

During the summer of 1983, they started a twice-monthly Monday residency at the Maple Leaf, alternating with the duo of John Magnie and Leigh Harris from Lil Queenie and the

Percolators, a prominent local band at the time. The shows were intimate, and since they were on Mondays, it never got too crowded. At that point in the Radiators' career, they were starting to outgrow the Maple Leaf. It would be a few more years until they outgrew it completely, but shows featuring the full band were always packed, uncomfortably so when the school year was in session.

After skipping the MOMs Ball in 1981, it was made clear to me that I missed out on something special due to concerns about my love life. So the following Carnival, I made it a mission to make it to Arabi out in St. Bernard Parish to the Disabled American Veterans hall where the ball was being held during this period. I found out that the Radiators were actually the house band; the Rhapsodizers started the tradition partly because Ed Volker's sister was one of the instigators behind the event. I also found out that the band usually composed a song based on each year's theme (an early one, "Hard To Tell," became a regular part of their repertoire). Many years later, another MOMs theme, "Tattoo Who?" morphed into another krewe's theme and became "Snafu Who?" It also became a regular part of the band's repertoire.

Though the Radiators had already developed quite a following, the ball was still very much an underground affair. Tickets were not required, but we were advised that costumes were *de rigueur*. We were further informed that face paints and tie-dyed clothing do not qualify as a costume, nor does nudity; you had to wear a funny hat or a mask if you were going to arrive in your birthday suit.

We got out into the suburban parish about an hour before the band was set to start, which allowed us to get a look at the crowd before the lights came down. These were some serious freaks—all of the remnants of the still vibrant sixties crowd were there. The costumes were as impressive as any I had ever seen, although there was a fair percentage of the crowd that seemed to have just thrown something together before heading out.

We were very young in this crowd, but once the band started, nothing mattered besides the music. The band played until very late, as was their custom during Carnival, and the crowd was deeply committed to having a great time.

In the years since, as the Radiators became more popular, the ratio of fans of the band to those just came out to have a killer party has increased dramatically. But at my first MOMs Ball, no one seemed to care about the specifics of the music. There was no significant difference in the crowd density from the very front of the stage to the rear of the room. People weren't facing the band as is typical at a concert. They were dancing with crazed abandon all around the hall. There was more energy in that room than I had ever felt before. The atmosphere was positively electric. The band was on fire and the crowd, though not paying strict attention, responded in kind. Everyone was super-friendly, especially on the breaks between sets, and the scene outside in the parking lot was magical as it crackled with the same energy. By the time it was over, I was convinced Dave Malone was right—it was the best party ever. I haven't missed one since my first.

As more and more fishheads found out about the MOMs Ball, the nature of it began to change. After 1983, you could no longer walk into the hall without an invitation. Over the years, various strategies were employed to keep people from crashing the party, including special invitations, custom-made buttons, hand stamps and finally, wristbands. Dave Malone's girlfriend precipitated the change in 1983. She announced the location of the ball on WTUL, Tulane's student-run radio station, and what seemed like hundreds of college kids arrived in various states of inebriation without costumes.

By the summer of 1982, I was a full-blown fishhead willing to travel far from home to see my favorite band. Early in the summer I followed them to Chicago, where they played a lunch hour date outside the Tribune building downtown. The scene was positively surreal as a handful of New Orleans fishheads were joined by an even smaller contingent of local fans and some from as far away as Cleveland. It seemed we weren't the only ones willing to travel to see the band.

They also played two shows at a suburban bar called Fitzgerald's in the town of Berwyn as well as an outdoor festival gig. All I remember about the festival gig was a very small crowd and Dave Malone adding a couple of choruses of Johnny Taylor's soul blues classic, "Who's makin' love to your old lady, while you're out makin' love" to their newest rave-up, "You Can't Take It With You." That song, which grew into a much-loved classic, was written for the many fishheads in Tulane's graduating class of 1982. Incidentally, there have been many medleys associated with that song, but I never heard "Who's makin' love to your old lady, while you're out makin' love" again.

By the time the second semester rolled around in 1983, the World's Fair was on everyone's mind. Officially known as the Louisiana World's Exposition, it was scheduled to run from May 12 until November 11, 1984 on reclaimed riverfront space in downtown New Orleans. Anticipation in the local press and among culture lovers across the city was running high from the moment that New Orleans was selected as the U.S. site. It reached a feverish pitch six months before the gates were set to open.

The city was determined to use the World's Fair as a giant tourist magnet, pulling first time visitors to the city from across the globe and enticing them to return again and again to re-visit the magic. The goal was nothing short of creating a sensational event that rivaled anything the country had ever seen.

The French Quarter, then mostly a dying residential neighborhood, was spruced up with new sidewalks complete with brick crosswalks, and the citizenry was primed for this important six-month long celebration. A new festival located in and named after the historic neighborhood was conceived as part of a strategy to get locals to visit the district and spend money in the restaurants, bars, and shops. However, very few locals actually went to the French Quarter Festival that first year.

The economy had been in a bust phase since the 1970s recession began and the oil boom, which left much of the gulf coast flush with cash, had ended. Inflation was causing economic hardships across the land. Clubs in New Orleans actually had discounted "recession nights" to try to lure locals to part with their hard-earned but recession-depressed dollars.

Amid all the anticipation over the fair, there were rumbles of discontent among both the citizenry and the many planners and organizers. The single day admission price, fifteen dollars, was deemed excessive. Cries of racism emitted from the black community that feared being left out of both the dollars to be earned from lucrative contracts and access to the event itself.

I GOT THE FISH IN THE HEAD

During the early planning stages of the fair, there was one decision that struck the music community in particular as completely ill advised and poorly thought out. The planned giant open-air amphitheater, to be built on the banks of the mighty Mississippi for big-time touring bands, was designed as a temporary facility that would be torn down at the end of the fair's run.

Amid plans in the early twenty-first century to further open up the river to the public is the design for a giant open-air concert space that would be located on the downriver side of the French Quarter. Imagine how different the touring calendar for concerts in New Orleans would have been if they had just built the amphitheater as a permanent structure.

Other civic leaders suggested that the estimates of out-of-town visitors were grossly exaggerated considering the state of the national economy and the simple facts of the summer weather in New Orleans. These dire predictions proved to be prophetic at the end of the six-month run when the organizers revealed that the only day that the fair hit its expected daily average attendance was the much-hyped opening day.

Despite negative talk from some quarters, expectations were high for music fans and local musicians. The fair took a page from the New Orleans Jazz and Heritage Festival and was designed to showcase the talents of Louisiana artists as well as national and international stars. The organizers suggested that there would be "at least fifteen stages" in addition to the amphitheater. The event promised to be world class in every way.

I immediately bought the season's passport, which allowed unlimited entry to the site that ran from Poydras Street to the uptown end of the Morial Convention Center. The season passport holders were among the few groups connected to the fair that ended up giving high marks to the event.

The music press began soliciting for performers for the World's Fair in late 1983. Jed Palmer, the former owner of Jed's University Inn on Oak Street, one of the Radiators' regular venues in the late 70s and early 80s, decided to get back into the promotions game and started a new business, Jed's Lookout, on the top floor of the Federal Fiber Mills building. He was aggressive with his advertising, taking out full-page ads hyping the new venue months before opening.

While the promised fifteen stages never materialized, there were still considerable options for hearing live music at the fair on a regular basis. Sheila's, an Australian-themed club on Fulton Street, featured the Neville Brothers every Wednesday night during the entire run. But my favorite venue presented non-stop music courtesy of a lazy-Susan-style stage that was configured to allow two bands to be set up at the same time. When the first band's allotted time was up, they simply rotated the stage 180 degrees and the next band, which had been setting up behind the curtain, cranked up.

One particular evening when the Radiators were booked onto this stage, a weak cover band was playing before them. They were doing a lame version of "Mustang Sally," a song that was a favorite when covered by the Rads. They were also playing overtime. The Rads were set up and ready to go on the other side of the circular stage. The stage manager set the thing turning and as the sound switched to the Rads, they picked up right in the middle of "Mustang Sally."

Despite the fact that music lovers truly enjoyed the six-month event, the abysmal failure of the Louisiana World's

I GOT THE FISH IN THE HEAD

Exposition left an open sore on the business climate in New Orleans in general and the music scene specifically. Jed's Lookout and Sheila's managed to stay in business for a while after the fair closed, but it was many years before the Warehouse District emerged as a trendy neighborhood.

The giant space that the World's Fair occupied remained pockmarked with blight for a decade as the financial debacle wove its way through the courts. The Riverwalk Marketplace was virtually the only bright spot in the area until new renovation added more condominiums, bringing upscale residents and the businesses that cater to them. However, the Riverwalk did not open until 1986.

The Wonderwall, an architectural and artistic marvel that was the whimsical heart of the fair, was dismantled and sold piecemeal at auction. Elements of its pastel-painted art deco design are still visible in some neighborhoods around New Orleans. The monorail and the M.A.R.T. gondola (Mississippi Aerial River Transit) were supposed to become part of the area's transportation infrastructure when the World's Fair closed. Needless to say, there is no monorail in the Warehouse District, nor is there currently a gondola over the river.

The city of New Orleans and its Downtown Development District and the Arts Council of New Orleans tried gamely to keep the musicians employed with the continuation of the Brown Bag concerts at noontime in the Central Business District and the French Market concert series. But the population exodus that began with the oil bust continued virtually unabated and affected every aspect of the business community.

A RADIATORS RETROSPECTIVE

In terms succinct but a tad bit overblown, one local publication called the year after the World's Fair "the bleakest musical period since the Beatles single handedly destroyed the Crescent City's recording industry in 1964." For music lovers, the worst part of the financial meltdown was the closing of Tipitina's. The last show at the iconic uptown club was in June 1984, just as the fair was opening. Though the ownership at the time blamed the fair, other issues were certainly at play.

While the closing of Tipitina's was a blow to the music community, it hit me and my friends in a more primal way. We had virtually grown up in the place. After a series of epic nights, one of my roommates from college called it "the greatest indoor spot on the planet." Luckily, I was consumed with graduate school and a research project that had me doing a considerable amount of traveling. In December 1984, after a couple of horrific trips to Michigan in the dead of winter, I landed a plum assignment—two weeks in southern California.

For a variety of reasons, my peer group held a mythic view of the west coast. A large percentage of my friends moved to San Francisco after college in part to be closer to the hippie ethic that defined us. Perhaps the feeling is best summed up in these lyrics from "Estimated Prophet," by the Grateful Dead:

> California, a prophet on the burning shore
> California, I'll be knockin' on the golden door
> Like an angel, standin' in a shaft of light,
> Risin' up to paradise, I know I'm gonna shine

I GOT THE FISH IN THE HEAD

A week or so after my work trip was scheduled, the Radiators announced that they were going to California for the first time. I was going to be in Los Angeles for their first shows on the west coast! However, I was living a strange reality. I had cut my hair for work and was spending large amounts of time in a suit and tie driving rental cars to interview executives in the offices of large corporations. I was twenty-three years old.

The first show in California was a happy hour gig at the Lighthouse, a club in Hermosa Beach that was famous among jazz lovers for a series of live albums by the likes of Lee Morgan, Grant Green, and Elvin Jones. Unfortunately, when the Rads played there at four p.m. on a Friday afternoon under a gray winter sky, it was virtually empty. I had driven like a maniac from a research interview in the San Fernando Valley in order to make the gig on time.

Later that night, they played for the second time in the Los Angeles area. This gig was even worse. They were the last group on a multi-band bill, and their set was cut short because of the two a.m. curfew. After countless nights where the band played until four a.m. or later, I had that Wizard of Oz feeling: "We're not in Kansas anymore." The following night was in San Diego, and I was able to structure my work schedule so that I had to be there as well. That gig, at the Belly Up Tavern in Solana Beach, represented pure redemption after the first two shows. They had a decent crowd and they tore the roof off the place. The Radiators eventually built up a strong following in northern California; the same cannot be said for Los Angeles.

A little over a year after the World's Fair closed, on the last weekend January of 1986, the music community celebrated the much anticipated grand reopening of a renovated Tipitina's. The first show was two nights before Super Bowl XX, which Mike Ditka's Chicago Bears won over the New England Patriots at the Louisiana Superdome. It had been eighteen long months. The new owners removed the drop ceiling, added a balcony, and for the first time, the club was air-conditioned.

All of the stars were in town for a three-day extravaganza leading up to the Super Bowl, and Tips was ready with three nights of great music. Friday night, Deacon John's New Orleans Rhythm and Blues Review hit the stage early, and the night didn't end until the wee-wee hours. The Dirty Dozen Brass Band opened the show.

Deacon John's great band backed an A-list parade of the stars from the 1950s including Ernie K-Doe, Johnny Adams, Jean Knight, Jessie Hill, Barbara George, and Earl King. After King's incendiary appearance, a jam session materialized. Art Neville took the stage and raised the intensity level through the roof with his spirited vocals and swelling organ. But the highlight of the early morning set had to be an unannounced appearance by Stephen Stills. He sang his classic "Love the One Your With" to great applause from the die-hards who refused to leave until the last note was played. Of course, I was in that number.

The locals in the sold-out crowd loved the club's new and improved layout. Tipitina's s now had two bars allowing for much quicker beverage service. The bathrooms impressed everyone, but the balcony is what really got the tongues wagging. The club just seemed so much bigger and the upstairs space provided respite from the crowds below.

I GOT THE FISH IN THE HEAD

Saturday night's act was the Radiators, who were celebrating their eighth anniversary together. They tore through three sets of fishhead music to the delight of many of the out-of-town visitors. The backstage was crawling with celebrities including Dennis Quaid, Timothy Hutton and two members of the Super Bowl's television broadcast team—Terry Bradshaw and Ken Stabler. Stabler, clearly enamored with the band, stood against the balcony rail right over Ed Volker's piano rig as the band played a new song, "Molasses." Bradshaw fell asleep in a folding chair right behind him.

The final night of the weekend featured the Neville Brothers. They took the stage to a sold-out house of football fans celebrating the big game that had ended just a few hours earlier. The energy was palpable. A new era in New Orleans music had begun. The best thing about the new and improved version of Tipitina's is that somehow, against the odds of encroaching commercialization, the vibe in the place didn't change. The energy that was so profound in the first incarnation didn't flag one iota. It was the same place, only different.

Around the same time, the Rads won a best of the unsigned bands contest, and it appeared that they were on the verge of signing with Epic Records. They were poised to spread fishhead music over the FM airwaves of America, and I had a flashback to the night before they left town for their first show in New York City a few years earlier. I had pilfered a sign from a mom-and-pop boudin shop somewhere in the country west of New Orleans. I made a dozen or so copies and pasted them all over the Dream Palace, including on Dave Malone's microphone stand. The sign read, "Are you carrying your spare radiator? Don't leave town without one."

A RADIATORS RETROSPECTIVE

Curiously for casual fans of the band, they shifted gears during the summer of 1986 and began playing acoustic shows. The first regular acoustic gig began a monthly series of Tuesday nights at Snug Harbor. Snug Harbor is the premier jazz club in town, and it was odd at first as most of the other patrons were expecting a sit-down show. Each evening began with everyone seated and by the end of the show nearly everyone was up and dancing to the fishhead beat.

That summer, I returned to Chicago, ostensibly to attend the Chicago Blues Festival, which "coincidentally" overlapped two Rads shows at Fitzgerald's in Berwyn. I had already begun underestimating my obsession for the Radiators in a vain attempt to avoid having my passion compared to the one-track mindset of a deadhead.

The Blues Festival immediately invited comparisons to the New Orleans Jazz and Heritage Festival. Though the lineup was quite strong, and included New Orleans acts like Dr. John and the Neville Brothers along with Chuck Berry, Otis Clay, and numerous others, the festival was nothing like the Jazz Fest. By the end of the weekend, my friends and I started calling it, "the disappointment festival." The sound was poor. It was free, but the space was inadequate for the size of the crowd that showed up each day.

But what was most troubling was the fact that no one carried around annotated schedules or even seemed to know who was playing. We took to asking random strangers, "Who's playing?" and we got the same blank stare and shoulder shrug from everyone. This mass group ignorance included moments late in the day when the biggest names in Chicago blues were on stage. We all realized how good we had it with the Jazz Fest in New Orleans.

I did, however, make one colossal error in judgment while in Chicago. I left early on Saturday night, before Chuck Berry closed the festival for the day, to get to the Rads show in Berwyn. I found out later that night that my guitar hero, Keith Richards of the Rolling Stones, jammed with Berry, one of his musical heroes.

In 1987, fishheads were elated with the news that after a long convoluted courtship, the band had signed with Epic Records. However, we slowly began to realize that an era had ended. By Mardi Gras 1988, driven by radio airplay of "Like Dreamers Do," the first single off of *Law of the Fish*, print media attention and a video on MTV (which was followed by a second of "Suck the Heads"), shows became incredibly crowded. What had been our little secret for a decade was now fair game for the masses.

In October 1988, I lit out again to see the band on the road. This time the destination was Minneapolis. Three years earlier, a group of dedicated fans had formed the Krewe of DADs, which was modeled after MOMs, and I wanted to see what the fuss was all about. The DADs ball was held in ballroom of the Hyatt hotel. One thing stands out about the trip and illustrates the contrast between the two balls.

We had a room in the hotel, and I brought a huge supply of Mardi Gras beads to hand out during the show. I was dressed in a store-bought costume from J.C. Penny that their marketing department had dubbed E-Gad-Zilla—the Party Dinosaur. It was made of bright green felt complete with huge feet and a gigantic, goofy-looking headpiece with protruding teeth and bulging golf-ball eyes. I draped a half-dozen silver beads around my neck and headed downstairs to check out the setup an hour or so before the music was scheduled to begin. The room was empty except for Kenny, the band's longtime soundman, when another guy walked in wearing the exact same costume!

We greeted each other with amazement, and I immediately tried to give him some of my beads. He repeatedly refused to accept them. All I could gather was that he thought I was giving away something of value even as I tried in vain to explain that I was from New Orleans and had a whole gross of them upstairs. I finally gave up trying when he suggested that if he took the beads no one would be able to tell us apart. Needless to say, I never saw him again.

During the summer of 1989 I traveled to Cleveland for the wedding of a friend from Tulane. At the reception something happened that demonstrated the power that the Radiators' music had over my friends and me. The couple had hired a pretty decent local rock band to play the reception. They were working fairly hard playing Santana covers and similar songs on a warm afternoon, but no one hit the dance floor except for the requisite wedding dances between the bride and her father and other family members.

But when the groom put on a bootleg tape of the Radiators performing Bob Dylan's "You Ain't Goin' Nowhere" during the set break, literally all of the guests in our age group crowded the dance floor shaking our butts like we were back at Tipitina's. When the chorus came around we all sang the line, "one of these days, my bride's gonna come" in unison at the top of our lungs. The band sat on the side in total disbelief.

I GOT THE FISH IN THE HEAD

On September 13, 1989, the New Orleans Artists Against Hunger and Homelessness staged their latest benefit concert. This time around it was at the Municipal Auditorium, and they had the best lineup in the history of the event.

The Dirty Dozen got everyone going before the Neville Brothers took over the stage. Then Allen Toussaint and his band featuring the guitarist Scott Goudeau followed. Toussaint's shows during this period were often hit-or-miss affairs that sometimes smacked of Las Vegas-style shtick. But this was an all-star review, and Toussaint only played three songs before bringing up the special guests. Irma Thomas, Rita Coolidge, and Boz Scaggs each took turns in the spotlight. The backing vocalists sang each singer's name as they came out amid a rising crescendo from the band. All three sang songs penned by Toussaint.

The great guitarist and producer Ry Cooder was up next. He played a short solo set and then he brought out Aaron Neville for a duet. The star power was increasing with Dr. John and his band due up following Cooder. The Good Doctor reprised "Makin' Whoopee," his hit with Rickie Lee Jones, with Rita Coolidge singing Jones' parts. It was a great moment. The Radiators closed the whole thing out, but their appearance was anticlimactic, and much of the crowd left while the fishheads danced the night away.

The Radiators eventually recorded two more records with Epic before the relationship ended. During this period, they toured extensively, opening up new markets all over the country. Their absence from New Orleans was an opportunity to branch out into the deep waters of New Orleans music. I had admittedly been mostly a one-trick-pony with a laser focus on the Rads. The night before Mardi Gras in 1990 sums up the intensity of this period. The evening started at Tipitina's where Snooks Eaglin was opening for the Radiators. The Rads' bassist, Reggie Scanlan, has a serious resume playing with blues and R&B artists both before and during his tenure with the band. He played with Professor Longhair in the 1970s and with the great, unsung bluesman Boogie Bill Webb in the late-1980s and up to his death in 1990.

Scanlan was backing up Eaglin along with the drummer, Oliver "Li Li" Alcorn. They tore up a great set that included a Mardi Gras Indian song medley that fit the occasion perfectly. I had a group of out-of-town friends in tow, and we left just as Tipitina's was getting packed with drunken tourists waiting for the Rads. We had big plans all over town. The first stop was Jimmy's, where the subdudes were playing. Unfortunately they were on break. We hung around for a while before the clock beckoned us to move on.

The next stop was the State Palace Theater on Canal Street, where the latest version of the Meters (George Porter, Jr., Leo Nocentelli, Art Neville, and Russell Batiste) was headlining a multi-band show. It was only the second time that this new lineup of the seminal funk band had performed. Though the timing of performances can be random and haphazard during Carnival, we arrived right on time. The theater was not overly crowded and after a quick stop at the bar, where vendors were selling t-shirts that pictured an eerie-looking, afro-wearing skull emblazoned with the words, "The Meters Will Funk You to Death," we headed onto the dance floor. It was almost as if the band was waiting for us to arrive. Within seconds they broke into "Smoke My Peace Pipe," another song inspired by the Mardi Gras Indians, and the first song of the set.

The Meters played a killer show and at three a.m. we headed back to Tipitina's for the third set of the Radiators. One of my friends from out-of-town on his first visit to New Orleans thought he was experiencing déjà vu. No, I said, you *have* been here before—five hours ago for Snooks. The Rads ended at five fifteen on Fat Tuesday morning. It remains one of the most amazing nights of music I have ever experienced.

Tulane remained a source of new fishheads all during this period. The band was often booked to play on the main quad, and the old-time fans could literally watch the *nouveau fishe* being spawned. All you had to do was look around and spot a couple dancing ecstatically or a lone male staring with his mouth wide open during one of Camile Baudoin's searing solos. I coined this look, "the drop jaw effect."

The Krewe of SNAFU, a group of hardcore fishheads from Tulane, held their first show at Tipitina's in conjunction with graduation festivities in 1990. They hosted another show on Halloween night. It was the beginning of a renaissance for the Rads since they were energized by this group of students who were heavily interested in the history of the band and songs from their earliest period. Members of the krewe began requesting songs that were long out of rotation and the band willingly obliged by resurrecting the ancient gems. I can take partial credit for this—at this point I had a vast collection of bootleg recordings of the band, although I kept them separate from the rest of my tapes. Two of the principals in the new krewe were friends, and I introduced them to some of the oldest recordings.

SNAFU shows became the latest sensation in the growing pantheon of epic shows. The band was truly energized by this latest wave of young fans, and the performances impressed even diehard original fans like me. The krewe set the stage for nearly a dozen other smaller groups to emerge over the ensuing years that hosted private parties featuring the Radiators.

Though the Epic years were over, the three-album run ended with *Total Evaporation* and their shot at the big time appeared to be over, the Radiators were reinvigorated throughout the early 1990s. The jam band movement was blossoming and a whole new generation of music lovers was drawn to fishhead music. The Allman Brothers and the Grateful Dead, masters of the loose-limbed groove, recognized them as kindred spirits. I got phone calls from friends excitedly informing me that the Dead were playing the Radiators' music on their set breaks and Bob Weir, the Dead's rhythm guitarist, began joining them on stage in San Francisco. Also, groups like Widespread Panic, Phish, and Blues Traveler, still relative youngsters, were unabashed fans of the band.

They were not playing all that much in New Orleans during this period, so homecomings, especially around Jazz Fest and Mardi Gras, were significant events for their local fans. Late in the 1994, Alison Minor, one of the driving forces behind the Jazz and Heritage Festival and a tireless advocate for the musicians of the city, was struck with bone cancer, and several benefits were organized to aid her in paying her medical expenses. The most impressive with respect to musical talent was held on January 11, 1995, at the House of Blues.

I GOT THE FISH IN THE HEAD

The Rebirth Brass Band, a group Minor was representing, opened the show with a short energetic set. Then Willie Tee hit the stage with Alfred "Uganda" Roberts on percussion and Steve Masakowski, from Astral Project, on guitar. They played a few of Tee's songs, and then Big Chiefs Monk Boudreaux and Bo Dollis came out. Tee was the mastermind behind the Wild Magnolias' legendary recordings that mixed the Indian rhythms with 1970s era New Orleans funk. Together with the Big Chiefs, Tee proceeded to re-create history. Yet there was no saxophonist; Tee's brother, Earl Turbinton, was a crucial part of the old recordings, and he was sorely missed.

Despite his brilliance, Earl Turbinton suffered through a range of personal and medical problems that came to a head during this period. Arriving home at three in the morning with a friend in late 1994, we heard Turbinton on WWOZ. He was on the radio for over an hour, alternating between playing solo saxophone and ranting and raving about Jesus and his love for prostitutes and other marginalized characters. It was completely over the top and the deejay, an inexperienced substitute, was overwhelmed and was unable to control the "interview."

On another occasion, Turbinton strolled into the trumpeter Kermit Ruffins' regular gig at Donna's with a snifter of brandy in one hand and his saxophone in the other. Seemingly high on himself, cocaine and/or alcohol, he approached the bandstand with nary a word to Ruffins. He just assumed that sitting in was his God-given right. When the time came for his solo, he was unable to generate enough saliva to wet the reed of his horn, a necessary step before playing the instrument. Without hesitating, he dipped the reed into the brandy glass, inserted it into the horn and proceeded to deliver one of the most incredible solos of his distinguished career. He then picked up the glass and walked straight out the front door without exchanging words with anyone in the bar.

The Radiators followed the Turbinton-less set at the Minor benefit. They did five songs including "Stop Breakin' Down," "Papaya," "Long Hard Journey Home," and "Like Dreamers Do" before George Porter, Jr. and Monk Boudreaux joined them on a spirited version of the Meters' classic, "They All Axed For You." The energy in the room was already cresting when the pianist, songwriter, and funk pioneer Eddie Bo took the stage with the augmented band. The Radiators know his music intimately, and Ed Volker ceded the piano to the legend and manned his percussion rig. Bo tore through a few songs with the Radiators wailing behind him before the sixties activist and poet John Sinclair hit the stage with poetry in hand. He performed his poem "Tommy Johnson" while the supergroup riffed on the blues classic "Spoonful." The finale was Kermit Ruffins and Corey Henry with Monk Boudreaux and the Radiators doing "Jump Back."

Nearly everyone who donated his or her time to Minor's cause had a personal relationship with her. She was a central figure on the scene for decades. Sadly, she passed away at the end of the year. The Jazz Fest honored her legacy by renaming the Heritage Stage, where interviews and intimate performances take place, after her.

The Minor benefit helped establish among the musical cognoscenti of New Orleans as well as the top-tier musical talents what the fishheads had been preaching for years. This was a band at the top of their game, firing on all cylinders and deeply tuned to the music of New Orleans. In can be argued that the extensive touring during this period negatively impacted their place in the musical pantheon of the Crescent City. But they were building the framework of hardcore fans and private parties that sustained them over the final chapter of their career.

Willie Green, the monster drummer from the Neville Brothers, occasionally sat in with the band, as did Dave Malone's brother, Tommy. But it was the guitarist Anders Osborne and his partner at the time, the vocalist and violinist Theresa Andersson, who became favorite guests while the duo was carving out a career in New Orleans beginning in the early 1990s. By 1996, they often joined the Radiators for the entire second set. Osborne's stellar slide guitar work neatly complemented the band, and everyone seemed eager to have the comely Andersson on stage. She added great backing vocals and sparred with the guitarists on her violin. So perhaps it was inevitable that the two Swedes would join forces with members of the Radiators in a supergroup of sorts.

Monkey Ranch played their first show at a dive bar in uptown New Orleans called Benny's on December 20, 1996. The band consisted of Osborne, Andersson, Dave Malone, and Reggie Scanlon of the Radiators, Willie Green on drums, Mark McGrain on trombone, and Glenn Hartman on keys. The show was a total free-for-all that lasted until five a.m. Modern-day bluesman Keb Mo played the whole second set instead of Malone. There were other sit-ins as well, including Tony Hall, who played both bass and drums. The set list was very loose with long wide-open jams and collaborative efforts on cover songs that all of the musicians had in common.

There were a few other performances by Monkey Ranch, but that first show was the kind of concert that musicians and fans alike dream of experiencing. There was no ego in the room, and the musicians were as enthralled by each other's music as the rabid audience. They stood by the side of the stage, itching for a chance to play as if they were school children waiting in line for the restroom.

It was also a wonderful last hurrah for a neighborhood bar that had nurtured members of the Neville family and countless other musicians. But the battle against gentrification was finally lost. The building that housed Benny's is now an upscale middle class home without so much as a sign indicating the significance of the corner of Camp and Valence streets.

The success of the amalgamated group had another significant effect: it opened the door for the first SuperJams presented by the newest promoters in town, a group of young uptowners with a fledgling business called Superfly Productions. Superfly went national with the Bonnaroo Music and Arts Festival and is now one of the premier independent production companies in the world.

When 1999 dawned, the musical denizens of the Crescent City and party people all over the world were faced with a conundrum. The financial and technological sectors of the economy were bracing for the then-unknown effect of a worldwide computer software glitch labeled the "millennium bug" or the "Y2K" problem. While the technocrats were preparing for a predicament that pundits were speculating could lead to the biggest meltdown in the short history of main frame computers, party planners and promoters were gearing up for the biggest event that the modern world had ever seen—the New Year's Eve countdown to the end of the twentieth century and the beginning of the next millennium.

The question that was on everyone's minds during most of the year was what will happen when all of the computer clocks, which were programmed long before anyone anticipated the transition from 1999 to 2000, switch over. Will there be widespread interruptions of financial markets, telecommunications, utilities, transportation networks and government services?

Given the status of the Crescent City as one of the world's premier party destinations, planning immediately got underway for the biggest New Year's Eve celebrations the city had ever seen. A member of the Krewe of MOMs that goes by the moniker the Royal Henchman conceived of an epic throwdown that he dubbed MOMs Millennial Madness.

It was going to be a pajama party for the ages with an open bar and sumptuous food in a setting directly across the Mississippi River from the city proper. Since I was now in a leadership role with the krewe I pushed for two of my favorite bands, the Radiators and Anders Osborne, as the featured entertainment.

Planners at every New Year's Eve event across the country were faced with the same problem. All of the expenses associated with throwing a party were extremely inflated given the unique nature of the occasion. There was also incredible competition among the various promoters for musical talent, and the decision was made early on in the year to extend an offer to the two bands.

The other side of the problem reflected concern about the Y2K bug. Though contracts were signed six months before the event, no one knew whether or not people would actually venture out of their homes. There was another issue for the krewe of MOMs party. Would people be willing to travel to New Orleans or would the fear of massive disruptions in air travel dissuade fans of the Radiators from traveling? There were clearly not enough local fishheads to support an event of this size. Only time would tell.

When New Year's Eve finally rolled around, all of the planning from the previous six months was put to the test. Besides the big event that the Krewe of MOMs had planned for the evening, most of the other venues in town had made extensive plans to celebrate the biggest calendar transition in our lifetimes. There were two schools of thought. Big hotels and larger clubs had elaborate arrangements that included an open bar and food. The prices were the highest the city had ever seen. All three Tipitina's locations were open with Kermit Ruffins and the BBQ Swingers in the French Quarter for $85, Cowboy Mouth at the Ruins for $100 and a triple bill of Gary Hirstius, the subdudes, and the Funky Meters at the uptown club for $115.

Storyville District, Quint Davis and Ralph Brennan's now-defunct club on Bourbon Street, had the Allen Toussaint Orchestra, Nicholas Payton's Big Band, Gregory Davis and Friends, and the Mahogany Brass Band for $195. The Red Room, the swanky nightclub on St. Charles Avenue, had Jeremy Davenport for $375. Mid City Lanes Rock 'n' Bowl had the Iguanas and Snooks Eaglin for $80. Superfly Productions booked Galactic and the North Mississippi Allstars at the Masonic Temple on St. Charles Avenue for $65.

More tourist-oriented locations upped the financial ante even further. The Hilton Hotel had Pete Fountain and Luther Kent for $425 or a suite for $1500. Harrah's Casino had the Neville Brothers for $200. The Hyatt had Fats Domino, Cyril Neville, and Eddie Bo for $200. Le Meridien had Marva Wright for $275. The House of Blues had Clarence "Gatemouth" Brown for $125.

Smaller clubs mostly opted out of the giant risk associated with high paydays for the musicians and a skittish public facing the unknown effects of Y2K. Margaritaville had Little Freddie King for free. Le Bon Temp Roule eschewed live music entirely and had a disco party scheduled. Jimmy's and Snug Harbor bucked the trend with George Porter Jr. for a mere $30 and Astral Project for $35, respectively.

Sweet Lorraine's decided to hedge; they advertised "a modest cover" but had no band listed. The Shim Sham Club, located where One-Eyed Jack's is today, hired the all-acoustic, no-microphones-used retro swing band the Asylum Street Spankers. With tongue firmly implanted in cheek, their ad stated, "When the lights go out, we'll still have the Spankers."

Of course, the lights didn't go out. In fact, given all of the apprehension leading up the switch from 1999 to 2000, nothing of any significance went awry in New Orleans, though there were some minor glitches reported across the globe. However, the fear of massive disruptions put a major damper on the size of the crowds at the various clubs and other venues. Most every promoter lost money and even the attendance for free events in the French Quarter was considerably less than in previous years.

A RADIATORS RETROSPECTIVE

I was blissfully ignorant of most of the developments since my plans for the millennium were determined when the krewe signed the contracts with the bands early in the year. The event at Mardi Gras World was first class in every way. We dined, danced, and drank in our pajamas. Anders Osborne put on a great set with Kirk Joseph of the Dirty Dozen Brass Band on sousaphone an Kevin O'Day on drums before the giant gumbo pot dropped and the skies over the Mississippi River were lit by a spectacular fireworks display.

Immediately after the fireworks ended, we scurried back inside for the first of two sets by the Radiators. They opened with the standard "Auld Lang Syne" and before the evening was over they performed three songs by the Rolling Stones, including "Let It Bleed," "Sympathy for the Devil," and "Dead Flowers," the tune that started it all for me twenty years earlier.

Of course, the story does not end here. Since the beginning of the twenty-first century, the Radiators have generated new fans while continuing to astonish the oldest among us by adding new songs to the repertoire and performing with unparalleled vigor. Though we look upon the dissolution of the group with decidedly mixed emotions, we know that experiencing the joy of their music and sharing the love in the community that they created has been a rare privilege. We are forever grateful to have been along for the ride.

Beginning shortly after its inception, the band distributed a newsletter called the Fish Headlines, which featured the upcoming schedule on the front page along with a fanciful drawing. The inside pages featured merchandise for sale on one side and a news section, which was usually written by Ed Volker. It was often whimsical and quirky reflecting the madcap imagination of the band's fearless leader.

The legendary "Fishhead Manifesto" was just one of his many creative gems that appeared in the Fish Headlines. I had the privilege of writing the news in the issue that was dated March/April 1988.

WHAT'S HAPPENIN'

March 12 marks the much anticipated release of the RADs third album on Epic records. Aptly titled Total Evaporation, the disc contains thirteen gill-tingling tracks spanning much of the band's illustrious career.

The disc includes several classics from the fishy past, a platter full of recent rave-ups and a Sadie-twisting hybrid teaser. It also features the multi-talented blowing of the Memphis Horns on three funky tracks and a sweetly unexpected total acoustic turn on "Molasses."

Reports from around the Crescent City and spanning the seven seas tell tales of lines forming at neighborhood record shacks everywhere. So, don't delay, catch the current downstream to yer local wheeler-dealer and get your fins on a copy today. Buy one fer yer mutha, buy one fer yer father, buy one fer yer sisters and yer bruthas!

I GOT THE FISH IN THE HEAD

WHAT'S BEEN HAPPENIN'

Over the past several months the funny fishy fellows have been playing with hollow instruments, sitting on stools again. That's right, a spate of acoustic shows have already occurred and hopefully more are soon to come.

Recent acoustic sightings include an intimate show in Aspen, Colorado, a couple of nights at good ole TIPs and two nights at The Bottom Line in the Big Apple. Spies from the East report a wide array of photographic gear was on hand on the second night. Further investigations confirmed the filming was for a TEE VEE show in the land of Kamikaze, that's right Japanese TV!

WHO BEEN HAPPENIN'

Fishheads at the recent show in Memphis, Tennessee, were pleasantly surprised to witness a special guest jammin' with the boyz in the band. Jim Dickinson, producer-extraordinaire of the new disc, notorious night-warden of the underwater zoo, and man about town, played the B-3 organ side-by-side with Zeke for most of the show. Yes indeed, what a sight, some wide grins sure were glowing that night!

The jam was such a blast that Jim hopes to put in a repeat performance at Jazz Fest come early May. So get your tickets in your hand, slide on down that mighty river, put on your tattoo shoes to dance and prance till you experience TOTAL EVAPORATION!

In April 1989, I began keeping a music journal that I called "Up
Front and Center," based on my favorite spot to listen and dance to
live music. The idea behind the journal was to keep track of informa-
tion about the shows that I attended since my goal was to become a
music writer. The first piece I had published was in Offbeat magazine.
However, I did not get paid for it. This is the first story that I got
paid for, which appeared in the lagniappe section of the New Orleans
Times-Picayune on September 4, 1992.

"Hot Combo for Labor Day"

At first glance, the schedule for WWOZ's upcoming Labor Day
benefit looks straightforward enough—the usual crew of be-
nevolent musicians giving their time and effort to help support
the community station.

However, headlining the event is an act, which may seem to
be an unlikely combination. New Orleans Rhythm and Blues
legend Eddie Bo is scheduled to close the day's activities with
three members of the Radiators as his backup band.

Eddie Bo is best known for a series of R&B hits in the 50s
and 60s, including the party favorite "Check Mr. Popeye." This
particular tune was one of a series of " Popeye" songs, which
were part of a dance craze during that time period. He is also
known as the man who at one point had more top 10 hits than
the prolific Fats Domino.

When Bo was first approached by Ruth Carlton of WWOZ
he was ready and willing to donate his time to the station. But
he told Ruth that he needed a backup band. While he was not
entirely familiar with the Radiators, he was ready to give it a
shot.

Carlton next approached Reggie Scanlan, bassist for the Radiators; when he was offered the chance to play with Eddie Bo, he jumped like Popeye reaching for his can of spinach. "Bo was one of Ed's (Volker, main songwriter and guru behind the Radiators) main composing influences coming up in the late 60s and early 70s," Scanlan said. "In fact," he continued, "We still cover a few of his songs every now and then."

While Scanlan cites most of his influences as being bass players and drummers, he does include one pianist on the list. "Fess (Professor Longhair AKA Henry Roland Byrd) played a big part on my musical development." he said with a tone of reverence for the godfather of New Orleans music. In fact, Scanlan played in Fess's band for nine months in late 1977 and early 1978.

When Scanlan approached his bandmates drummer Frank Bua and singer/guitarist Dave Malone to join him on the gig, they both reacted enthusiastically. And so a band was born, if for only one day.

New Orleans music buffs with excellent memories will recall that Bua was featured in the seminal early seventies band the Dogs. This group also included two other future Radiators, Ed Volker on piano and Camile Baudoin on guitar. Interestingly enough, their first demo tape from 1971 included a version of Eddie Bo's "Tell It Like It Is," which is not to be confused with Aaron Neville's classic by the same title. Bo's song, according to the man himself, was written, "a few years earlier" than Neville's standard. So a line up of musicians that seems a bit unlikely at first proves to have some rather interesting roots. The Radiators have moved beyond the New Orleans sound, which defined their selections of cover material as a young band. But they remain loyal to those tunes and players who had the greatest influence.

Eddie Bo is most certainly one of those influences. Eddie Bo is a man not given to flashy self-promotion. At a recent gig he chatted in a down home style with any and everybody, including those who approached him and those who did not. He conveys an air of self-satisfaction off stage and a humble dignity befitting a musician who has been active over four decades.

Once he hits the stage, Eddie Bo the Performer takes the forefront. He calls out tunes with a seasoned expertise and sings and plays in a style musicians 30 years younger would envy. During his second set he gave up his piano to fellow musician Richard Knox, who sat in for one tune. While Knox jammed on a boogie-woogie medley, Bo was up on the center of the bandstand, singing, dancing and waving his handkerchief like it was Carnival Day. When asked if he planned a rehearsal for the upcoming benefit his brief reply was, "Nah." To which he added after receiving a quizzical look, "Don't need to." Indeed, Bo is a man who has earned the respect of the toughest critics in the world of music, his fellow musicians and songwriters.

A month after the piece appeared in the Times-Picayune, I began sub-mitting unsolicited stories to the paper. The idea was to write about was happening in the music clubs of New Orleans. I titled each sub-mission "Clubland." This article was written in October 1992. It has never been published before.

One of the most exciting things about the club scene in New Orleans is the frequency of guest appearances during shows around town. Musicians in this area have a great deal of respect for each other and are quite often personally or professionally related. A popular act, both local and nationally touring ones, inevitably draws a number of players eager to check out the latest sounds. The richness of this musical scene translates into a plethora of late night jams, impromptu reunions between former bandmates and guest artists sitting in for a tune or two.

There is also a family connection here that goes beyond the well-known groups whose music is literally a family affair. The Neville Brothers are a household name, the Batiste Brothers are becoming more and more well known and the Marsalises are building a jazz dynasty. Yet, there are dozens of lesser-known siblings and other relations playing music in and around the New Orleans area.

For the Malone family, the last month or so has seen an-other of the semiannual reunions between brothers Tommy and Dave. Dave is the singer/guitarist for the Radiators and younger sibling Tommy is the singer/guitarist for the sub-dudes. Whenever both bands are in the city its a pretty good bet that Dave will jam with the 'dudes or Tommy will sit in with the Rads. Or as is usually the case around Jazz Fest, they'll both show up to play with each other's bands. After all, they've been playing together since high school in Edgard, Louisiana.

The August 19 subdudes show at Tipitina's was no exception. During the second set, Dave joined his brother on stage for some harmony vocals on the subdudes original, "Straight Shot." You could see the communication between the two brothers as they both wailed the song's chorus, "Straight shot, keep crying for my mama."

That show also featured sax men Joe Cabral of the Iguanas and ever-ready horn man Jerry Jumonville sitting in with the 'dudes as well. Joe has done some studio work with the Subdudes and Jerry has played with everybody!

On August 29 Dave Malone celebrated his fortieth (not fifty-second, as was reported by the only daily in town) birthday, and Jerry Jumonville was again in the house at Tips. This evening, as the Radiators had a parade of guests cross the stage during their second set, Jerry got a mic stand and joined the band. The Radiators were really cooking as they celebrated their singer's milestone and Jerry's long, breathy solos added heat to the fish fry.

Also joining the band for a song was guitarist Johnny Price, who sang a rave up version of "Mustang Sally," and Tipitina's MC Ricky Castrillo. Ricky borrowed lead guitarist Camile Baudoin's axe and added some of the sonic texture that he is making famous with the Observers. Meanwhile Camile switched to two hubcaps adding a percussion groove to the party atmosphere on stage.

As if that jam was not enough, the band scaled back to the core six and invited gospel singer and Tip's doorman Jo

"Cool" Davis up on stage. Jo left his post at the side door briefly enough to raise the roof with an exquisite rendition of the Curtis Mayfield classic "People Get Ready." WOW!

Newslines was a column that appeared in Tower Records Pulse!
Magazine, which was distributed internationally by the record store
chain. I was a regular contributor between 1996 and 1998.
The following are excerpts that appeared in separate issues in 1997.

Under the pretense of giving a speech to induct **Allen Toussaint** into the Rock 'n' Roll Hall of Fame, **Quint Davis**, the producer/director of the New Orleans Jazz and Heritage Festival, was lured to Tipitina's for a star-studded surprise 50th birthday party.

Ed Bradley of 60 minutes fame and **George Wein**, the executive producer of the New Orleans Jazz Fest and the Newport Jazz Festival, led a roast. **Jimmy Buffett** was unable to attend but sent a videotape instead.

The musical entertainment featured numerous jams and special guests. **Kermit Ruffins** and the Barbecue Swingers led things off in a traditional jazz vein and were joined by clarinetist **Dr. Michael White**, trumpeter **Gregg Stafford** and singer **Wanda Rouzan**.

Mardi Gras Indians **Bo Dollis** and **Monk Boudreaux** presented Davis with a beaded jean jacket and were joined in traditional Indian chanting by **Allen Toussaint** on piano and **George Porter, Jr.** and **Brian Stoltz** of the **Funky Meters** on bass and guitar respectively. Then singers **Irma Thomas, Marva Wright**, **Raymond Myles** and **Wanda Rouzan** joined in.

As the night progressed, **the Radiators** hit the stage and were joined by former member of the **subdudes**, **Tommy Malone**, for a forty-minute set. The climax of evening was a performance by **George Porter, Jr. and the Runnin' Pardners**, which featured guest appearances by **The Dixie Cups** and **Chris Owens**.

I GOT THE FISH IN THE HEAD

Solo Fish: Singer/songwriter/keyboardist **Ed Volker** of the **Radiators** has been performing solo acoustic much more frequently as of late including a recent performance at Snug Harbor Jazz Bistro. The staid jazz club is a far cry from the sweaty dance fests that are his bread and butter with the fishhead funk of the Radiators. Joining Volker on the intimate stage at "Snug" was **Joe Cabral**, one of the saxophonists for the **Iguanas**. The two traded licks on standards such as "Mack the Knife" and eclectic originals that don't fit the in the Radiators' repertoire. The Rads will be celebrating twenty years as a band this coming January and are touring in support of their compilation, *Songs from the Ancient Furnace* (Sony/Legacy) whenever Volker isn't tickling the ivories at some jazz club.

*From 2002 through 2004 I was the editor of an ambitious monthly
publication called* Beat Street. *Each issue was dedicated to
a specific topic. The following two pieces were published in the
issue featuring the Radiators.*

Rads Time Line

Pre-history

Before forming the Radiators, all of the members of the band
had well-established track records performing with each other
and with other musicians. Bassist Reggie Scanlan logged time
backing up Professor Longhair and James Booker among others. At the time of the band's formation he was performing
with guitarist/vocalist Dave Malone in a band called Road Apple. Keyboardist/vocalist Ed Volker, lead guitarist Camile Baudoin and drummer Frank Bua had been performed together
since the late 1960s. Their outfit at the time of the band's
formation was called the Rhapsodizers. They had a significant following and occasionally served as Earl King's backing
band.

January 28, 1978

The five original members join forces for the first time at Ed
Volker's garage on Waldo Drive in Gentilly. The first song they
play together is Van Morrison's "He Ain't Give You None."
It continues to be a staple of their anniversary performances.
The five recognize their musical camaraderie immediately and
begin the process of ending their other commitments and putting together the Radiators.

I GOT THE FISH IN THE HEAD

The band hones their chops at weekly performances at Luigi's, a pizza parlor on Elysian Fields Ave. The location is currently a restaurant known as Bud's Broiler. The Wednesday night shows were free and a cult following began to develop revolving around the freewheeling atmosphere. Eventually they simply outgrew the space, which had no raised stage.

They also begin to develop a reputation playing marathon three-set shows at venues across town including Tipitina's, the Maple Leaf Bar and a long-standing Saturday night gig at the now defunct Dream Palace on Frenchmen Street. Their fan base that began with University of New Orleans students expands to include students at Tulane and Loyola Universities, local residents and out-of-town visitors who encounter them during Mardi Gras and at the New Orleans Jazz and Heritage Festival.

February 14, 1980

The band cuts their first recording, a 45 RPM single of their double entendre paean to crawfish eating—"Suck Da Heads and Squeeze the Tips, Parts 1 and 2." It was recorded live at Luigi's. The illustrious Bunny Matthews provided the artwork for the record sleeve.

May 8, 1980

The band records their first full-length release, *Work Done on Premises*, at Tipitina's. This two-record set establishes a precedent by being the first official live recording from Tipitina's and the first local band to ever release a double album complete with gatefold. It was released on the band's label, Croaker Records.

A RADIATORS RETROSPECTIVE

1981

The band releases their second 45-RPM single "My Whole World Flies Apart" backed with "Join the Circus."

January 1982

Their first full-length studio album, *Heat Generation*, is released on Croaker Records.

March 1982

Percussionist Glenn "Kul" Sears begins sitting in with the band. Before the year is out, he becomes an official member of the band.

Summer of 1982

Ed Volker, Reggie Scanlan and Glenn "Kul" Sears form the offshoot band Blind, Crippled and Crazy. The trio plays regularly at the Maple Leaf Bar and Tipitina's as well as elsewhere around New Orleans. It was one of many side projects featuring members of the band that continue to this day.

The Epic Years
1986

The band signs with Epic Records, a subsidiary of major label CBS.

1987

Epic Records releases *Law of the Fish*, the first of three albums for the label. They produce two videos that appear sporadically on MTV. The first, for the single "Like Dreamers Do," was filmed at Tipitina's and in an undisclosed location in the swamps surrounding New Orleans. The second video, for the song "Suck Da Heads and Squeeze the Tips," was filmed at a seafood joint on the Lakefront in New Orleans East. It featured a crawfish feast and the incongruous image of bandleader Ed Volker dripping crawfish juice down the ample cleavage of a model from Los Angeles while a recipe for boiling crawfish scrolled up the screen. The video was quickly dropped from rotation when a national call-in resulted in the video being voted "trash"—the other choice was "smash." Both videos are collector's items today.

1988

The Fishing Line is established to allow fans across the country to call for concert updates. It was followed by a BBS and eventually a full-blown web site that can be accessed at www. Radiators.org.

The Radiators appear on a special MTV broadcast from the French Quarter during Mardi Gras featuring Tracey Ullman, Buster Poindexter and Cajun chef Justin Wilson.

The Radiators cut a television commercial for Budweiser.

May 8, 1988

The Radiators appear live from the Ritz in New York City on the King Biscuit Flour Hour.

1989

Epic Records releases *Zig-Zaggin' Through Ghostland.*

A RADIATORS RETROSPECTIVE

1991

Epic Records releases *Total Evaporation*.

1992

The band ends their relationship with Epic Records following a buyout of CBS, the parent company of Epic, by Sony Records.

The band releases their second live recording *SNA-FU—10-31-91* culled from a private party recorded at Tipitina's on Halloween of that year. The Krewe of SNAFU continues to present private parties each year during the Jazz Fest.

1994

The band records their third live album, *Bucket of Fish*, at the historic World Theater in St. Paul, MN.

The band appears on the *Late Show* with Conan O'Brien.

May 1, 1994

Glenn "Kul" Sears plays his last show with the band at the New Orleans Jazz and Heritage Festival.

1995

New Dark Ages is released on What Are? Records (see following page for example of press materials)

1996

Sony Legacy releases the budget CD *Party On*, which included cuts from the Epic years. For a short time, it is available at truck stops everywhere.

I GOT THE FISH IN THE HEAD

1997

Songs from the Ancient Furnace—the Best of the Radiators is released on Sony Legacy.

August 28, 1997

The Radiators appear on Louisiana Jukebox on Cox television in New Orleans.

1998

The band releases *Live at the Great American Music Hall.*

October 2001

The band travels to Europe with nearly 100 fans in tow. The unique arrangement allows the band to break into new markets with a guaranteed crowd at each venue.

2001

The band releases *The Radiators*—their most recent recording on Rattlesby Records.

January 28, 2003

The Radiators celebrate 25 years together. This rare feat in the world of rock 'n' roll is even more impressive considering that they have played close to 3,500 shows with the same original lineup of musicians.

Special thanks to the following individuals for their assistance in putting together this time line: Reggie Scanlan, Tony Zucker, Paul Toracinta, Karl Bremer, and Chris Weddle.

THE RADIATORS HAVE GOT YA COVERED

Just when you think you've heard it all, up bubbles another obscurity into the set list. Here's but a handful of songs from the bottomless bag of tricks the Rads bring to the bandstand:

Spencer Bohren *Straight Eight,* O. V. Wright *I'd Rather Be Blind, Crippled & Crazy,* Credence Clearwater Revival *Green River*, Jelly Roll Morton *Don't You Leave Me Here,* George Clinton & P-Funk *Take Your Dead Ass Home*, The Doors *Soul Kitchen,* Blind Willie McTell *Brokedown Engine*, John Lee Hooker *I'm In the Mood*, Staples Singers *I'll Take You There*, Big Mama Thornton *Just a Little Bit*, J. J. Cale *Magnolia,* Al Johnson *Carnival Time*, Jimi Hendrix *Are You Experienced*, Chris Kenner *I Like It Like That,* Jesse Winchester *Isn't That So?*, Jimmy Reed *Baby What You Want Me to Do?,* Tom Waits *Heart attack and Vine,* Tim Hardin *If I Were a Carpenter,* Curtis Mayfield *Pusherman*, Taj Mahal *Railroad Bill*, Sleepy John Estes *Everybody Ought to Make a Change,* Rolling Stones *2000 Light Years from Home*, War *Cisco Kid,* Professor Longhair *Cry to Me,* Carl Perkins *Honey Don't,* Neil Diamond *Solitary Man,* Mississippi John Hurt *My Creole Belle,* Chuck Berry *Nadine*, Patsy Cline *I Fall to Pieces,* Mose Allison *Parchman Farm,* Van Morrison *He Ain't Give You None* (first song played as the Radiators), Muddy Waters *Catfish Blues*, Little Feat *Sailin' Shoes*, Robert Johnson *Dead Shrimp Blues*, Fats Domino *Let the Four Winds Blow*, Zombies *She's Not There,* Al Green *Take Me to the River*, Merle Haggard *The Bottle*

I GOT THE FISH IN THE HEAD

Let Me Down, Bob Dylan *Subterranean Homesick Blues*, Bo Carter *Pig Meat Is What I Crave*, The Who *Magic Bus*, Willie Dixon *Howlin' for My Darlin*, Dave Mason *Feelin' Alright*, Allan Toussaint *Sneakin' Sally Through the Alley*, Ray Charles *Tell Me How Do You Feel?*, Fred Neil *The Other Side of This Life*, Robert Parker *Barefootin'*, Blind Willie Johnson *Everybody Ought to Treat a Stranger Right*, Louis Jordon *Chick's Too Young to Fry*, Roky Erickson *I Walked with a Zombie*, Meters *They All Asked for You*, Doc Pomus *Lonely Avenue*, Frank Zappa *Trouble Comin' Every Day*, Leiber & Stoller *Love Potion #9*, Bobbie Gentry *Ode to Billy Joe*, Mississippi Fred McDowell *You Got to Move*, Hank Williams *Lonesome Whistle*, Moby Grape *Murder in My Heart for the Judge*, Eddie Bo *Tell it Like It Is*, Ahmet Ertegun *Mess Around*, Johnnie Otis *Willie & the Hand Jive*, Donovan *Season of the Witch*, Stevie Wonder *He's Misstra Know It All*, Beatles *Tomorrow Never Knows*, The Band *Up on Cripple Creek*, Smokey Robinson *Tears of a Clown*, Grateful Dead *Deal*, Rev. Gary Davis *Cocaine*, Eric Von Schmidt *Turtle Beach*, Wild Magnolias/ Willie T *Firewater*, Mabel Godwin *Ling Ting Tong*, Captain Beefheart *Grow Fins*, Count Five *Psychotic Reaction*, Rufus Thomas *The Dog*, Joseph Spence *And We Bid You Goodnight*, James Brown *Doin' It to Death*, Smiley Lewis *Down the Road I Go*, Johnny Cash *I Still Miss Someone*, Leadbelly *Relax Your Mind*.

This story was the cover feature in An Honest Tune—the Southern Journal of Jam. It appeared in the Summer 2004 issue.

Forefathers of Jam—The 25-year Escapade of the Radiators

When the five members of the Radiators took the stage at Tipitina's on January 22 for the first of a three-night stand at the venerable club they were celebrating 26 years of making music together. Incredibly, the band is composed of the exact same five guys that jammed together for the first time in a New Orleans garage 26 years earlier.

Let's put that in perspective—over a quarter of a century of regular touring, some 3,700-plus performances, with the same personnel. The Grateful Dead changed keyboardists approximately every ten years. The Rolling Stones lost a founding member in less time than that. Let's not even discuss the personnel changes in the Allman Brothers.

Obviously, the Radiators are not in the same league as those three bands. But if their claim to fame was merely their longevity, you would not be reading this article.

So how do you explain a band that has consistently been lauded by the critics, were selected as one of the best unsigned bands in the land in 1986, has amassed a rabid fan base that certainly rivals any other in terms of dedication and commitment, yet remains mostly under the radar of the current generation of jam band fans and the mainstream media? You start at the beginning.

When keyboardist and principal songwriter Ed Volker, front man/guitarist Dave Malone, lead guitarist Camile Baudoin, bassist Reggie Scanlan and drummer Frank Bua played their first song together, Van Morrison's "He Ain't Give You None," on that fateful January day in 1978, they were already seasoned musicians.

Volker, Baudoin and Bua were core members of the Rhapsodizers, a band that turned some ears during their brief tenure in the mid 1970s. Malone and Scanlan were bandmates in another outfit called Road Apple. Scanlan had also done stints with legendary New Orleans musicians James Booker and Professor Longhair.

All five musicians felt the musical connection immediately. What started as a one off jam session became a lifelong journey. The Rhapsodizers and Road Apple were quickly disbanded and the new group, the Radiators, began to take life.

The music they played was an amalgamation of their combined musical experiences. Volker mined the deep vault of New Orleans songwriting, dredging up classics from the era when the studios of New Orleans ruled the world and transformed the blues of the Mississippi Delta and Chicago into psychedelic excursions. Songs like Robert Johnson's "Dead Shrimp Blues" and Huey "Piano" Smith's "I Hear You Knockin'" became staples of their live sets in those heady early days.

Malone brought a more contemporary perspective to the proceedings. His influences run the gamut from the Beatles to Credence Clearwater Revival with a healthy dose of Memphis soul and gritty R&B thrown into the mix. Classic three-minute singles like Martha and the Vandella's "Dancing

A RADIATORS RETROSPECTIVE

In the Streets," Van Morrison's "Moondance" and Clarence Carter's "Slip Away" were transformed by Malone's impassioned vocals and the combined energies of the band into something else entirely.

While exciting new arrangements of cover songs have been a central part of the band's appeal from the beginning, the songwriting of Volker instantly raised them into another realm. Within two years of the band's formation, the first batch of new originals were recorded live at Tipitina's and released as a double album called *Work Done On Premises.*

It was considered a bold move in 1980 for a young band to release an album without the support of a record label. Prior to that, their only recorded effort was a 45-RPM single of "Suck Da Heads and Squeeze the Tips," their classic double entendre ode to the New Orleans passion of eating crawfish.

The decision to self-produce and release these recordings with little or no distribution or label support foreshadowed developments a decade down the line when they would again attempt to handle the business themselves.

In the meantime, the Radiators were developing their fan base in New Orleans. The band's unique approach to cover songs combined with their stunningly arranged originals and D.I.Y. attitude led to a problem that has plagued musicians for time immortal—pigeonholing. What kind of music do you play? We play fishhead music! Well, what's fishhead music? Come to Luigi's on Wednesday night and find out. A genre and a moniker for the fans were born.

In those early days, that pizza joint near the lakefront of New Orleans was the epicenter of the world of the Radiators.

The Wednesday night gigs were free, the beer was cheap and the three set shows lasted until 4 a.m. The first regular fans came from the nearby University of New Orleans.

For a band that famously never rehearsed, Wednesdays were the unofficial rehearsals. They would try out new songs and get their groove on. The space was so small, there was no stage at all, that when it got crowded the front row was practically in the middle of the band.

As the word about the band spread and the fishhead community began expanding, they simply outgrew Luigi's. But the impact of those few years continues to affect the group. Song favorites like the seldom-heard original "Texas Chainsaw Massacre," a hard charging guitar tour-de-force that features the twin guitar attack of Malone and Baudoin mimicking the sound of a menacing chainsaw, which segues into the Meters' classic "Cissy Strut," exposed another key appeal of the group—the jam.

When the Radiators were formed, there was no such thing as a jam band. The term wouldn't arise for at least 15 years. Of course, there were precursors to the style and elements of the Grateful Dead as well as the Allman Brothers that crept into their mix from the beginning.

Songs that the Dead covered have long been part of the extensive repertoire of the Rads as well as the shared penchant for free form jams. There is little doubt that the original lineup of the Allmans, with the twin guitars of Dickey Betts and Duane Allman, also influenced the Radiators' development.

But there was also something else that made them a band apart from other acts in the pre-jam band community. Regardless of their influences, their instantly telepathic rapport, and their individual abilities, the Radiators are and have always been a New Orleans band. The fact that they share a lineage that goes back to the very beginnings of American music cannot be overstated.

As the Radiators began to make in roads into other sections of New Orleans through regular gigs at the Maple Leaf Bar and Tipitina's, they began attracting a different sort of fan. Tulane University became the center of a new group of fishheads dubbed in some circles as the "nouveau fishe." Regular performances, beginning in 1982, on the quad in the center of the school's uptown campus provided a steady stream of new fans.

They were music lovers from out of town who were less versed in blues, R&B and New Orleans soul and more in tune with what is now defined as "classic rock." Whether a re-worked arrangement of the Rolling Stones' "Dead Flowers" or a scorching version of Bob Dylan's "All Along the Watchtower," the Radiators' repertoire seems to have something for everyone schooled in 60s and 70s rock 'n' roll.

But for many of those fans, individuals who thought that "Iko, Iko" was a Dead song before they were exposed to Mardi Gras in New Orleans, the Radiators provided a musical education unlike any available then or today (for a list of the 1,320 songs the band has played go to www.ancientfurnace.net). Obscure blues and country musicians, much of the British Invasion, sixties psychedelia, nearly the entire canon of New Orleans R&B from Earl King and Professor Longhair to Eddie Bo and Champion Jack Dupree, the classic songs of Bob Dylan, and early rock 'n' roll from the likes of Little Richard and Carl Perkins were all part of the course work that took place in clubs all over New Orleans.

By 1984, the first cohort of Tulane fishheads had matriculated and many of them left the city with racks of bootleg cassette tapes of the band's live performances. These recordings, most fully sanctioned by the band, became the blueprints for the Radiators forays in the wider world.

The home cities of that first wave of fishheads to leave New Orleans after college became the first places that the band began spinning its collective web. Appearances at the original Lone Star Café in New York City set the stage for the group's first foray into the record business. They signed a deal with Epic Records that would result in three recordings, beginning with 1987's *Law of the Fish*.

But the record industry at that time was in a state of great flux. The relationship with Epic soon soured amid allegations that the label wasn't doing enough to support the band. But truth be told, the label never really got a grip on what the Radiators were all about.

The Epic years never yielded a hit. Two videos were made, "Like Dreamers Do" and "Suck Da Head," from *Law of the Fish*. But the production values and concept for both were ludicrous. They were quickly relegated to the circular file receiving very little airplay.

The second problem with their major label tenure was the recordings themselves. Similar accusations continue to plague bands that the mainstream media can't pigeonhole. But the fact remains—the intensity of their live performance was never successfully captured in the studio by Epic despite their enlisting well-respected producer, Jim Dickinson.

Since the Epic years, the Radiators have released a number of decent recordings on independent labels or on their own label, Croaker Records. But by and large the mainstay of their career has been the live show.

They have seriously devoted followings all across the country and in several European countries. Many of these fans are so faithful that they have formed "krewes" modeled after the Carnival organizations in New Orleans particularly the infamous Mystick Krewe of Orphans and Misfits (MOMs) for whom the Rads have functioned as house band for the entirety of their existence. These krewes throw semi-private (knowing someone is usually enough to gain admittance) parties where all bets are off and the hardcore fans relish in unbridled musical energy and obscure set lists.

However, amid all of the focus on the live performance the songwriting of Ed Volker often gets overlooked. His songs, of which there are said to be thousands unrecorded in addition to hundreds in the band's repertoire, take their cues from the greats. He is capable of writing catchy ditties that would not be out of place on the pop charts, searing indictments of the status quo that could just as easily be defined as protest songs and introspective tunes that explore the inner life, soul and spirit of mankind.

Critics have claimed that Volker wears his influences on his sleeve, but what they are usually unaware of is the depth of his songwriting and the role the rest of the band plays in perfecting the work. His original songs that enter the permanent Rads canon have been vetted to a degree almost unheard of in pop music. The way in which the band manipulates the arrangements until they are as tight as the proverbial drum resemble nothing but the way jazz musicians are able to dance within and around a standard while making it their own. Oftentimes a song is re-worked, its lyrics re-written and its tempo adjusted until it reaches a zenith.

Once a song, and this goes for a percentage of the covers as well, enters the rotation, it is not immune to further manipulation. Consider the opener at the 2004 MOMs Ball, Earl King's classic "Come On." Better known as "Let the Good Times Roll," this song has been covered by Jimi Hendrix and Stevie Ray Vaughan among others. In the hands of the Radiators, the simple genius of King's tune mutated into a roiling, greasy, nearly unrecognizable alternative version. Fans are already labeling it "Come On, Part 3" in a dual homage to King's original and the creativity of the Radiators.

For fishheads, the Radiators have always been about the songs. But an element of their fascinating synergy that bears mentioning is the musicianship within the band. From those early telepathic experiences comes a veteran group of musicians that communicates with pure musical energy.

Baudoin's guitar work has always generated serious ear candy. His solos run the gamut from searing grease to manic shredding. He plays with a lyrical intensity that comes from being a musician's musician—he hears everything that is happening on stage.

Malone has always relished the front man role and in the early days his guitar playing was merely adequate for a singer.

But as the years have past, his ability, passion and technique have literally leaped up the ladder putting him on the top rung of lead singer/guitarists performing today.

Scanlan and Bua are locked so tight as a rhythm section that they have redefined what it means to be "in the pocket." Sometimes on stage, when it seems that the band is about to fall out and loose the groove (something that happens very rarely these days even though they continue to take great musical chances), Bua and Scanlan are all the other three need to find their way back.

What can you say about Ed Volker? Known over the years in various guises, he is the muse behind the band. His keyboard work has also grown over the years and he seems to know intuitively exactly what touch is right to put a particular song or musical moment right over the top. His manic stage antics mask a serious musician and songsmith with a depth rarely seen among so-called pop musicians.

In a perfect world, the Radiators would have released an album a year over these 26 years. There would have been experimental recordings along the lines of Volker's unsung solo effort, *Lost Radio*. There would have been collections covering everyone from Bob Dylan to Blind Willie McTell. Baudoin and Malone could easily have released a series along the lines of Frank Zappa's *Shut Up and Play Your Guitar*. But more importantly, the hundreds of Volker originals that were played a few times and then dropped out of regular rotation would have lives all their own.

But this is not a band that dwells on what was or what could have been. They leave that up to the fans. They have soldiered on through attempts at self-management, business decisions that were poor in retrospect and a steady stream of marginally acceptable agents and other support entities.

The band now finds itself on the cusp of a new day. The anniversary shows back in January were recorded for a live CD/DVD project and from all accounts the performances, including guest turns by Gregg Allman, Karl Denson and a host of their New Orleans musical compatriots, were among the most incendiary of their career.

What is most telling about the Radiators is the constant growth within the band. Volker continues to come up with genuine gems. His rapport with Malone, who has regularly functioned as his alter ego with respect to lyrical content, has never been more complete.

Even the choice of covers, which one could easily assume would be relatively static after 26 years of playing together, continues to expand with a sensitivity to the proclivities of the audience. In recent years, The Who's "Magic Bus" and Talking Heads "Burning Down the House" have entered the repertoire shocking and delighting longtime fans.

On stage, they continue to amaze and astound. Exponential growth in musicality is common among young bands as they develop, but for a group that has been together for 26 years to continually experience the joys associated with finding new common ground among themselves and their audience is nothing short of magical.

I wrote this bio of the Radiators in 1992. It was targeted to the media in Europe and was commissioned as part of a distribution deal to get the Croaker recordings (Work Done on Premises, Heat Generation, *and a new addition,* SNAFU-Halloween 1991) *on the market overseas after the band left Epic Records. Variations on the first sentence have been used by countless other writers to explain the band's origins. I am proud to have written it.*

The Radiators were born during a transitional time in the history of New Orleans music. The seminal funk band, the Meters had recently broken up, only to spawn the Neville Brothers. Professor Longhair, the spiritual embodiment of Crescent City soul, passed into the next world during the first month of the 1980s. A decade that would prove to be a fertile period for the development of a unique blend of sounds that could only be labeled "fishhead" music.

Because of an American obsession with categorizing and pigeonholing music, the nascent band was faced with the problem of how to market and promote this sound. Because of the eclectic mix of musicians and styles of music within the band, they defied definition within the usual parameters of American music. They weren't quite soul or R&B, they definitely were not a blues band despite having blues influences. And they didn't really consider themselves to be a rock 'n' roll band. Thus Croaker Records was born.

By 1983, the self-owned label had produced three separate efforts in an attempt to get the music to the people. The first was a single of their now classic double-entendre ode to the New Orleans passion of eating crawfish, "Suck the Heads."

Recorded live at Luigi's, the single demonstrated the unique blend of songwriting and rhythmic patterns, which would define their sound.

The second release was a monumental success in capturing the band in the live setting, a two-record set recorded at Tipitina's in May of 1980. *Work Done On Premises* accomplished much more than it set out to and now stands as a historic testament to the potency of the band before they ever ventured out of New Orleans.

The third release on Croaker records was the eagerly anticipated, at least by the now burgeoning legions of local fans, studio debut. Entitled *Heat Generation*, the disc showcases the songwriting talents of the group's leader, pianist Ed Volker and the shimmering duel guitar work that has become the trademark of the band.

The mid-80s were a period in the band's history, which solidified their now national fan base. Through 1984, they played marathon three set shows till the wee hours at various local nightclubs and during short ventures within the region. However, the legend of their live shows was preceding them to places like New York City and Minneapolis, Minnesota, to Boston and Washington, D.C. Carried home by students attending Tulane University and by music aficionados visiting New Orleans for Mardi Gras and the Jazz festival, the word spread across the country. The early fan base has now multiplied and the successes of those early shows have been magnified and intensified to near cult status.

By the late 1980s, this underground scene finally came to the surface and attracted the attention of the mainstream record business in the United States. During their tenure with Epic records, the band released three albums, recorded a pair of music videos, which received airplay on Music Television, were broadcast playing live numerous times in the New York area, and continued to produce new music while touring the country playing their now legendary live sets.

Since leaving Epic, Croaker Records has reemerged as the vehicle for distribution of the band's recorded material. In addition, they have added another collection to the catalog, which takes their recorded output to another level. Captured live at Tipitina's, *SNAFU-Halloween 1991* is a recording, which exemplifies and demonstrates what the dedicated legions of fishheads have known all along. This new release of incendiary jams, which includes a number of cover songs paying homage to the band's musical heroes, is slated, along with the entire Croaker catalog, for release in Europe in 1993.

This bio was part of the press package that was written by the booking agency Skyline Music in 2001. It retains the original formatting.

The Radiators

Against all odds, the Radiators have kept their original line up together for 25 years, bringing their New Orleans- infused blend of swamp rock and rhythm and blues to fans throughout the United States and Europe. With a constantly changing "book" of more than 300 original songs, as well as hundreds more covers, the Radiators never play the same show twice. As a result, they are followed around the country by a devoted group of "fishheads", who use meetings at live shows, as well as the internet to discuss various aspects of the band's music.

As the Radiators' sound and stage show have been influenced by jam bands of the sixties and seventies such as the Grateful Dead and the Allman Bros. Band, so have younger jam bands of the nineties and beyond listed the Radiators as a major influence. Members of Phish, Blues Traveler, Spin Doctors, Widespread Panic and Gomez have paid tribute to the Radiators in interviews and on stage.

With their eponymous twelfth release (their sixth complete studio album), the Radiators have made what may be their

best album ever. Although it is rare for rock and pop musicians to take a step forward once out of their twenties, the Radiators have done just that, with the help of Grammy-wining producer Jim Gaines. Perhaps most famous for his work on Santana's Supernatural, Gaines has also produced and/or engineered work by acts as diverse as Blues Traveler, Journey, Huey Lewis, Sly and the Family Stone, Stevie Ray Vaughn, Luther
Allison, and Coco Montoya.

Gaines says, "I've wanted to work with the Radiators since I first heard their music in the eighties. They represent the best traditions of the hippie band. That's what made the Dead what they were. That spirit is what makes contemporary bands like Blues Traveler,
Phish and the Radiators so great."

The Radiators new CD contains twelve original songs that range from the moody intensity of "These Fugitive Dreams" to the funky feel of "Driver" to the country twang of "I Don't Speak Love." Look for adult alternative airplay as well as television and movie exposure.

The band consists of: Ed Volker, keyboards and vocals, founder and principal writer; Dave Malone, guitars, vocals and songs; Camile Baudoin, guitars; Reggie Scanlan, bass; and Frank Bua, drums.

A RADIATORS RETROSPECTIVE

Although the members have played as sidemen with New Orleans legends Professor Longhair, Dr. John, James Booker and Earl King, they are best known for their 25 years on the road and in the studio
as the Radiators.

After the run of three albums that the Radiators recorded for Epic Records ended, that label's parent company, Sony Music Distribution, continued to re-release the band's music from the three Epic albums. In 1996, they released a budget line compilation called Party On. *In 1997, they released* The Best of the Radiators—Songs From the Ancient Furnace. *I was commissioned by Sony/Legacy to write the liner notes. After two drafts, the label decided to go in a different direction. Here is the second draft. It has never been published before.*

Over the course of their storied twenty-year career, the New Orleans Radiators have been successful in the ever-volatile music business by doing what comes naturally. They have achieved unprecedented longevity for a rock 'n' roll band by building up a rabid fan base of like-minded music lovers who seek substance over style.

These fans, dubbed fishheads, started appearing soon after the band's inception in 1978. The first wave at a tiny pizza joint on New Orleans' lakefront led to a long-term relationship with the college crowd. Three generations of Tulane students have taken the bait since. Each has passed the baton as they graduated and each has taken the music back home. In the ensuing years, the Radiators have developed a following in virtually every state in the union.

The band is, and has always been, quintessentially New Orleans. Their sound is a crazy, indefinable jumble of rhythm and blues and rock 'n' roll with a healthy dose of blues and '60s-inspired psychedelia. There is even a little bit of country thrown in the mix.

From the outset of their career, the Radiators were besieged with demands that they define and pigeonhole the music. A task that is as impossible now as it was then. So they called it fishhead music.

A perfect name for a band unlike any other. They are a composite of individual players that combine to define "the whole is greater than the sum of its parts" maxim. The rhythm section of drummer Frank Bua and bassist Reggie Scanlan are locked so tight they may as well be brothers. They provide the rock solid foundation upon which the other band members groove.

Singer/guitarist Dave Malone and singer/pianist Ed Volker have forged a unique relationship in the ego-driven world of pop music. While Volker writes most of the material, he doesn't sing all of the songs. He shares the songs with Malone who, as his alter ego, brings a rock 'n' roll presence to the live show. Volker can write songs for his partner's vocal skills or he can choose to add his own whisky-voiced inflections to the stew.

What is fishhead music? People have been asking the question for as long as they have been staring, slack jawed, at one of lead guitarist Camile Baudoin's fiery solos. Trying to answer that question is like trying to teach a fish to fly. But central to the discussion is the songs themselves.

Volker, as principle songsmith, has written literally thousands of songs over his thirty-plus years of following the muse. The band itself, has a repertoire of original material that numbers in the hundreds, most of which can be performed with no rehearsals necessary.

A RADIATORS RETROSPECTIVE

Longtime fishheads wax nostalgic for songs that the band played once or twice back in say, 1982. They remember the words, when the band can't even place the tune! Fans have been responsible for "bringing a song back" into current rotation. The band has even had a rare rehearsal or two in order to "re-learn" a forgotten gem.

With an output as prodigious as their incendiary live shows, it's amazing that they have not released a recording a year since the band's inception in 1978. Conservatively based on twelve songs per CD, that would make their theoretical recorded output at around 225 songs. Yet because of the precarious whims of the ever-changing recording industry, the number immortalized on vinyl (and shiny metal) is considerably less.

What your holding in your hands is the first remedy of an oversight that is the fault of neither the band nor its fans. *Songs From the Ancient Furnace* is just that—a collection of some of the most memorable music that has ever crawled out of the dark, smoky places were it was born and nurtured to life. Songs that span the history of America's most enduring band.

All of the songs on this disc are staples of the band's fearsome live repertoire. Some pop up on set lists more regularly than others, but taken as a whole, the collection is representative of the synergy of the five players. For die-hard fishheads we have even included a killer live version of their classic ode to the foibles of romance, "Love Is A Tangle."

Six of the tunes, each and every one a serious crowd pleaser, have appeared on previous studio recordings. Eight are culled from various unreleased and outtake versions that never made it to the public.

91

I GOT THE FISH IN THE HEAD

Some, like "My Whole World Flies Apart" are old, from the humble beginnings when the band was satisfied with playing three nights a week in New Orleans. An early version of "Whole World" was their second single, released on 45 RPM, in the early '80s. A close look at the lyrics gives a hint about the importance of the fledgling audience to the band in the early years. "They play out their souls, but nobody knows until you walk through the door."

By the time they got around to writing songs like "L'il Paradise (sic)" an undulating ditty with a fabulous tropical groove, fans all over the country in spots as disparate as Madison, Wisconsin, and Boston, Massachusetts, were listening to their unique groove. A sound that was born and bred in the bars of New Orleans and matured on the vines of the ever growing fishhead family all over the country.

Of the six previously released songs, "Like Dreamers Do" is easily the most recognizable. It's a concert mainstay that never fails to get the crowd screaming when Volker launches into the signature piano riff.

"Doctor, Doctor," previously released on their first Epic CD, *Law Of The Fish*, demonstrates Volker's knack for visceral lyricism with lines such as "Just give me a fight, a foot of lead pipe and a ticket to New York." The song emerged at a time when the band was just beginning to spend extended periods on the road. It bears the true fishhead stamp with a rollicking chorus that has inspired countless late night sing-alongs.

Gritty lyrics also pop up on "Confidential," a song whose narrative details an elusive hunt for gainful employment. It chronicles the search with a catalog of fantastic characters who are all involved in some kind of low-down scandal mongering.

While the Radiators' lyrics often show evidence of serious eclecticism, Volker describes it more as a response to the freedoms generated during the sixties. That era gave rise to forms of music, which combined multiple elements, from the influence of surreal novels to the nonsense syllables of nursery rhymes.

That mixture of influences has also played a part in the various elements of the live show. It is the very same sensibility that allows the band to follow a Merle Haggard tune with something by Cream.

Like the era that spawned the group, many of their songs appear to contain incongruous elements. A song like "Let the Red Wine Flow" seems, on the surface, to be a paean to the party ethic that has been a part of the Radiators since their early days as the soundtrack to the Mardi Gras. But a closer inspection finds arcane lyrics that explore the mysteries of life.

Before "going unplugged" was the vehicle for jaded rock stars seeking to increase lagging record sales, the Rads were playing occasional acoustic shows. From the first, back to 1984, the rare acoustic performance has always been a chance for the band to let loose, swing out and play obscure songs.

Out of that carefree, acoustic mindset came the bittersweet ballad "Molasses." A great example of the collaborative nature of their songwriting, the lilting lyrics and melody are from the pen of Volker, and the guitar part was written by Malone. "Molasses" is a wistful, yet optimistic look at the difficulties of maintaining a spiritual connection from separate physical spaces.

I GOT THE FISH IN THE HEAD

While Volker's lyrics have never ceased to amaze the dedicated listener, it's his take on relationships between the sexes that holds the most validity to the widest audience. The title of one of the outtake versions presented here says it all. "Nail Your Heart To Mine," written way back in the day, sums up the immediacy of that heady period at the beginning of a new love affair.

In "L'il Paradise (sic)," Volker examines another aspect of relationships: the pitfalls of trying to control someone. It explores the gypsy mentality and is a realistic take on the futility of trying to tie another person down. The song seems to say that it is better to appreciate someone for who they are rather than attempting to change them into someone that you want them to be.

Relationships between individuals form the basis of many of the Radiators songs but "Zigzagging Through Ghostland," taken from their second Epic CD of the same name, deals with one of the true pitfalls of humanity at large: our penchant for conflict and war. It contrasts the evasive "zigzagging" tactics that Native American warriors used to evade the U.S. Calvary and the survival tactics of GI's in Vietnam.   Throughout his entire career, Volker has never been afraid to tell it like it is. "Fools Go First" is a jaunty crowd favorite that warns would-be suitors of the pitfalls of making the first move.

Out of all the songs that made the cut for *Songs From the Ancient Furnace*, "Fluid Drive" and "Fever Dream" stand out—each for different reasons. "Fluid Drive" is the rarest of all the tunes. It was written years ago, forgotten, brought back, forgotten again, and now is back for good on this collection. The band hasn't played it that much, but it's a great example of the Rads as up-tempo as they get.

"Fever Dream," on the other hand, is a fishhead favorite. Its lyrics tell of a spell cast upon the narrator that evolves into a fabulous jam.

The last two cuts on *Songs From the Ancient Furnace* are both signature songs that define fishhead music much better than any writer could. "Honey From the Bee" pulls you in with a catchy rock 'n' roll chorus, but the lyrics caution the listener of the hidden dangers of built-up expectations. The central image is one of simplicity. Take life as it comes and "Don't forget to get your honey from the bee."

"Law of the Fish" is a staple concert opener that takes the entire culture of the fishhead family and rolls it out with no holds barred. The version on this collection is an outtake from their first Epic album. It includes the now infamous "Gummin' Your Nub" jam that demonstrates the band's incredible ability to morph their own tunes.

When the Radiators first started recording back in 1980, they did something unprecedented and still not repeated to this day. With only one 45-RPM single, "Suck Da Heads," available to the public, with only two years tenure as a band, with a small, but increasingly loyal, fan base, they released a live album. Not just any live album, mind you, but a *double* live album recorded direct from the stage at the legendary Tipitina's.

It was that initial effort on their own Croaker Records that set the stage for all that would come in the future. The three albums on Epic, from which most of this material is derived, were just another step for a band that has steadfastly refused to compromise. They have followed their own path from the beginning and have carved their own niche.

They've been down, but never out. They have been vilified and deified. They've played for pennies and played for gold. Through it all, they have never, for nearly twenty years, stopped doing what they do. We are all the richer for it.

The Radiators 25th anniversary was celebrated at Tipitina's with two epic nights of fishhead music that were filmed in high definition and later released on the DVD Earth vs. the Radiators—The First 25."
I wrote this piece, which appeared in the liner notes.

Tulane Daze

Of the dozens of bands that performed at the weekly TGIF parties held on the Tulane University Quad in the 1980s, only two still exist—those keepers of the Uptown funk, the Neville Brothers and the New Orleans Radiators.

Fishheads that discovered the band after that fertile creative period marked by marathon three-set shows may be shocked at the atmosphere in those decidedly politically incorrect days. The first TGIF that I attended, in the fall of 1979, was a celebration of the 10th anniversary of Woodstock. 12 ounce cups of draft beer could be had for 25 cents. The beer was free if you dressed like a hippie. No one I knew had to dress up.

The Radiators were mainstays of the lively Quad scene. They played numerous times for the regular Friday afternoon affairs as well as at the WTUL Rock On Survival Marathon—an annual, weekend-long festival of live music dedicated to supporting Tulane's radio station.

At that time, college radio as it is defined today didn't exist. Much of the on-air programming at the station represented the best of what is now called "classic rock."

New Orleans was a different place as well, which was reflected in how people reacted to the music and the culture. The city had yet to be "discovered." There were very few sources for information about the city. Tourists were essentially restricted to the French Quarter, and the tourism market that currently drives the economy was in its infancy. All of the current land-marks on the music/culture landscape, such as the New Orleans Jazz and Heritage Festival and Tipitina's, were local phenomena or didn't exist yet.

For a Tulane student fresh off the plane from Long Island, New Jersey, Chicago or any of the other places where fishhead music would ultimately take root, hearing the Radiators was a profound revelation. As I matriculated both in my studies and my musical fixation, I would eagerly await the next Quad show because it would provide ample opportunity to meet new friends and initiate new fans. I remember numerous instances of what came to be defined as "the drop jaw effect." Awestruck kids standing in front of the stage with their mouths wide open.

When the band wasn't busy unwittingly tapping into a market of out-of-town students that would eventually spread the gospel of fishhead music all across the country, they were playing at small joints in New Orleans with the occasional big ticket show at the only "real" club in town—Tipitina's.

But the bread and butter, or should I say the oyster and hot sauce, of the band's schedule was the regular Wednesday night gig at Luigi's Pizza Parlor in the Gentilly neighborhood, home base for students at the University of New Orleans.

Members of the band have famously stated that they never rehearsed in the early days. They didn't have to. The Luigi's gigs felt like you were walking into the group's private rehearsal space. There was no stage, the band simply set up in a corner and when it got crowded, you were so close to the band that it felt like you were *in* the band.

A RADIATORS RETROSPECTIVE

For Tulane students, going to Luigi's was a trip, literally and figuratively. For new drivers in the Crescent City, it's a complicated haul all the way from Uptown to the Lakefront. There was also competition from the Boot—a student-oriented bar right off campus that featured 50-cent Highball Night on Wednesdays.

It wasn't easy to corral partners to head to the Lakefront even considering that the gigs at Luigi's were free and usually lasted until four in the morning. I remember too many nights spent trying desperately to get someone, anyone to leave the "safe" confines of Uptown and the Boot before finally giving up in the wee wee hours.

As the Radiators began developing a serious fan base, the urge to play out of town became stronger. Some of the first shows outside the city were on the Northshore of Lake Ponchatrain and on the Gulf Coast of Mississippi. At approximately the same time, the first cohort of Tulane fishheads began graduating.

They took the music, in the form of live bootleg tapes, most of which were fully sanctioned by the band, all across the country. When they returned home, forever changed by their experiences in New Orleans, they craved the same music performed live.

By 1984, the band was touring nationally, first to New York, then Chicago and Minneapolis. The first California tour, in early 1985, was a revelation. Imagine their reaction seeing faces from New Orleans at a seaside bar in Manhattan Beach—these people are everywhere!

I GOT THE FISH IN THE HEAD

Several years later, the Radiators, due in part to the exponentially spreading Tulane diaspora, were on the national map. A three-album deal with Epic Records cemented their role as the first rock band from New Orleans to develop a significant national following.

Thousands of performances later, there is still probably only two degrees of separation between every fishhead and Tulane University. And twenty-six years later, the process continues. Just as there were fishheads who graduated in 1979, there are fishheads who graduated last year.

I have often likened Tulane to a river that runs through New Orleans. Students from all over creation have flowed on that river since the school went national more than a century ago. The unique music and culture of New Orleans changed each and every one who managed to get out of Uptown and the Boot.

Some, like myself, clambered ashore and made New Orleans our home. But for thousands upon thousands of others, that river played a defining role in who they are as adults. But more significantly, it set the stage for how they define great music.

That definition is clear; it is the music that influenced the musicians in the Radiators when they were developing their unique sound—a rollicking mix of classic New Orleans, early blues, soul, R&B and even country with a heaping dose of psychedelia to keep it interesting.

It is also the songs. Hundreds of originals from the pen of Ed Volker and thousands of covers from the most diverse array of artists ever. If you can't find a song you like in their vast repertoire, you haven't been listening.

I wrote this piece in reference to the SNAFU show on May 1, 1997. The theme was "Leave the Planet." The show took place a month and a half after the cult called Heaven's Gate committed mass suicide by ingesting chocolate pudding mixed with Phenobarbital. The group, led by Marshall Applewhite, believed that a spacecraft was trailing the comet Hale-Bopp and it was going to take their souls to another level. Kingsley Stoken, one of the leaders of the krewe of SNAFU, made an announcement before he introduced the band for the second set. He said some chocolate pudding had surfaced at the party and he warned the crowd, "Please don't eat the chocolate pudding, the chocolate pudding is bad pudding." Of course, all the fishheads thought this was hysterical considering that we occasionally exhibited cult-like tendencies. A number of the songs that the band played that evening are referenced in the piece including "We Be Boppin'," "Knockin' On Heaven's Door," "Season of the Witch," "Ooh Poo Pah Doo," "Breezin'," "Swamp Rat," "Stealin'," and "Heavy Planet." Since the band was clearly in on the joke, they also played "UFOs Exactly" and in keeping with the custom established by the krewe of MOMs, a new song that reflected the theme. There are also other song references and a few inside jokes designed to amuse the krewe members.

I GOT THE FISH IN THE HEAD

A thin man with a manic grin and a breezin' blond walk into the Heavy Planet Cafe. "A large chocolate pudding, please!" he asks in a swamp rat voice. "And," she adds, "spoons for 500."
And so it began again. Snafu Who? Snafu You!
A wing ding King thing? A Glaus carouse? Stealin' back to my old used-to-be?

SNAFU-Situation Normal, All Fucked Up!
SNAFU-Sex, Narcotics And Fish Uphoria!

There are 20,000 freaks under the seas and they all arrive, some barely alive, some carrying flags, some wearing tags—fishheads and fess heads, MOMs and DADs, tadpoles and pollywogs, the reborn and the unborn, the pre-hysterical and the mystical, old money and nouveau fishe—all ready for the season of the witch!
There are parties and then there are PARTIES!
There is music and then there is MUSIC!
Combine the two with some festival goo, add a little Zigaboo, a dash of Oop Poo Pa Doo *(sic)* and the roots come home to roost. Yessiree Bob, Chocolate pudding and bananas—for 500!

Two trippin' chicks bust a move for the smokin' hole. One says to the other, "Man, I'm slippery when I'm wet." The second replies, with smoke in her eyes, "That's what you get when you been Hale-Boppin'!"

I wrote this press release for the Radiators European Tour in October 2001. It was commissioned by Clio Tours.

HISTORY & HERITAGE TOURS

For Immediate Release

Clio Tours Offers Unique Travel Opportunity for Music Lovers
100 Fans To Join the Radiators On Fall European Tour

New Orleans—June 20, 2001—Clio Tours, a New Orleans-based leader in the European travel industry, announces a unique travel opportunity for fans of the New Orleans Radiators. Through a joint agreement between the tour company, the band and its record label, Atlanta-based Rattlesby Records, 100 of their fans will join the band on an eight-day trip from the United States through four European countries.

This unprecedented opportunity is a venture bound to impress both the travel and music industries. Fans from various American cities including New Orleans, San Francisco, Denver and Chicago will join the band in New York City on Saturday, October 6, 2001. For the next eight days, the fans will be offered unique access to the Radiators. They will fly with the band across the Atlantic, stay in the same hotels, travel together in luxury coaches across the continent and gain admittance to a variety of special events designed specifically with them in mind. The tour begins in Brugge, Belgium, and includes stops in Amsterdam, Paris and London.

Andy Ambrose, the mastermind behind this unique concept, is the Director of Sales and Marketing for Clio Tours, a division of Stephen Ambrose Tours that specializes in music-related travel. He said, "Touring Europe has always been a high-risk venture for American bands without a significant following. By joining together with our tour company, the band significantly minimizes the financial risk associated with entering a new market."

Barney Kilpatrick, the president of Rattlesby Records, said, "This is a band that relishes the opportunity to interact with their fans. The trip also provides the band with a built-in audience for six concerts in unproven territory. He added, "For the Radiators, the opportunity to perform in some of the greatest cities in the world with their American fans in tow is a match made in heaven."

Besides unprecedented access to the band and all travel and lodging expenses, the tour price also includes one meal per day as well as laminate entrance to all of the shows. Additional perks will include custom T-shirts, laminates, invitations and other special incentives that will make the trip a tour to remember.

This piece was written about the European tour in October 2001. It has never been published before.

The Ugliest American in Paris

In early 2001, Andy Ambrose, Yakir Katz and I began hatching a plan to bring the Radiators to Europe. Andy and Yakir operated a tour business that catered to history buffs, which was founded by Andy's father, the esteemed writer and historian Stephen Ambrose. They had years of experience bringing large groups of Americans across the pond. I had extensive public relations experience and was well known among the loosely knit group of fishheads. They were going to put together a tour and I was going to use my expertise and connections to get a group of fans to travel with the band.

The idea was not original, other bands had subsidized their travel into new territory and minimized their financial risk by bringing fans along, but we felt that this experience would be unique. Also with a goal of recruiting seventy-five hard-core fans, the band was guaranteed a devoted audience at every stop. The trip was set up and advertised for October 2001. Six concerts over eight days in four cities were scheduled. Little did we know that on September 11, 2001, radical extremists would hijack four American airplanes, destroy two while bringing down the World Trade Towers in New York City, crash one in a rural area of Pennsylvania and the fourth into the Pentagon in Washington, D.C.

The trip was seriously in doubt less than a month before travel was to begin. Several members of the group bailed out as their fear got the better of them. The chance of generating any local interest in the European cities was doomed because advance publicity concerning nearly one hundred Americans traversing the continent in tour buses and by rail was curtailed due to the obvious threat of terrorist activity.

Despite these setbacks, the trip was a whirlwind of activity that gave me a healthy, newfound respect for the rigors of rock 'n' roll. I had followed the band to other cities before, but I had never traveled *with* the band other than a few short drives in the New Orleans area. After an overnight flight from Newark, we landed in Brussels, split into two groups, boarded two modern tour buses and headed straight to Brugge, Belgium, for the first night's concert. However, it was ten a.m. when we arrived in Brugge—way too early for us to check into the hotel.

Brugge is wonderful old-world city that is popular with European travelers. It's very picturesque with a main square so massive that the entirety of New Orleans' Jackson Square and the surrounding buildings could fit neatly into its center. We spent the day sleep-deprived before several cups of coffee revived us for the evening's concert. The Cactus Club was tiny. It was Sunday night in a tourist town. Without the American fishheads the place would have been virtually empty.

The Radiators are known for expressing their feelings in the set list—given the debacle associated with a sold out hotel and many complaints about lack of sleep, they opened the show with their composition "Nightmare on The Misery Train," which they segued into George Clinton and Parliament's "If You Ain't Gonna Get It On, Take Your Dead Ass Home." It was a one-set show that most everyone was glad was over given the jet lag we were experiencing.

Early the next morning, eighty or so haggard Americans boarded the buses for the drive to Amsterdam. The pace was non-stop since we had all of the band's gear with us. We had to get to the hotel, get the gear to the club for the sound check, get food and get to the show. We had a little time in the afternoon to check out the sights, but I began to understand why bands on tour rarely have any time for normal tourist-related activities. We just had to get to the show on time. They had to conduct a sound check and perform.

The Winston Kingdom was another tiny club off the beaten track near the red light district in Amsterdam. Many of the fans had indulged in the infamous pleasures of the hedonistic capital of Europe and the energy in the crowd flagged. The band, on the other hand, was on fire playing a long set that seem to improve exponentially as the evening progressed. As usual, they reflected the circumstances of the day in the set list. "Hard Rock Kid," with the line, "All the hoboes call him king," made an appearance as did Bob Dylan's, "Rainy Day Women #12 and 35," with the chorus, "Everybody must get stoned." The band had everyone singing along to the line, "I wanna join the circus, I wanna join the band," when they played "Join the Circus" in the encore.

No one felt that way the next morning when we had a seven a.m. call for the long drive from Amsterdam to Paris. Tensions were high on the bus since some of the group wanted to sleep and others wanted to listen to music. How the driver tolerated us, I'll never know. As we were approaching Paris it became apparent that we were late. Both buses drove to the club to drop off the gear before heading to the hotel in the 16th arrondissment.

The hotel was located in a Muslim section of Paris. This struck us as rather ironic. My roommate and I were shocked when it appeared that we had a single double bed to share. A mildly freaked out call to the front desk was met with typical French nonchalance and a hint of disdain, but at least the clerk spoke English. "Ah, monsieur you must pull the bed apart." Doing so left no room whatsoever for our bags.

We barely had time for dinner when it was time to head to the show at Chesterfield's. All of the tokers in the group, failing to realize that we were no longer in Amsterdam, lit up with impunity in the club. Though no one was kicked out, the word went out from the band's management that the following evening, smoking would not be tolerated and the bouncers would be searching everyone for contraband. We found out later that in France, if the police raid a club, everyone, including the employees and the band, goes to jail.

The trip was my first across the pond and most of my emotions as an American were centered on the reactions and treatment we would receive in Paris. I had heard all the stereotypes of Parisian arrogance and condescension for Americans, particularly of the "ugly" variety. With a full day to spend in the City of Lights, my friend and I were prepared for whatever the French threw at us.

We purposely dressed in a continental style to avoid the negative stares and rude behavior that we assumed would be part and parcel of the Parisian reaction. All over Paris we were greeted in such a warm fashion that we were left slightly confused. Finally we figured it out. With few Americans abroad, the initial assumption (before our bad French exposed us) was that we were German, Italian or British. After a wonderful day all over the French capital, we rejoined the group, which was loaded with individuals who could not have cared less about the ugly American stereotype. In their T-shirts and shorts they immediately conveyed their nationality. Tellingly, they were the ones who were less than impressed with Paris and the French.

True to their word, the staff was on point when the group arrived for the second night at Chesterfield's. Numerous members of the group either never got the word about the searches or ignored it. The men at the door were pleasant but thorough with the task at hand. By the time the whole group was inside, they had a full collection of paraphernalia including pipes, rolling papers, hashish and marijuana, which was placed in a large basket by the door.

The band was unfazed by all of the hullabaloo—it was just another night at the office for them. Yet they were positively energized by the day off in Paris. It showed with the first truly magical performance of the trip. They segued Little Feat's "Dixie Chicken" into "Goin' Down the Road and Feelin' Bad," and the whole group reveled in our deep connection with the band. They also played "This Wagon's Gonna Roll," one of their greatest "road" songs. By the first song of the encore, Volker's plaintive lament "Grief Snafu," the whole crowd was aching for something epic to close our first four days on the continent. We got it with a monstrous version of the Who's "Magic Bus." We were on a magic bus indeed.

The most surprising thing about that night happened as we were leaving Chesterfield's. A feeling of camaraderie had developed over the first four shows. Our group of fishheads was positively elated as we exited the club into a cool, foggy Parisian night. Standing by the side of the front door were two smiling employees. In one of the Frenchmen's hands was the basket of paraphernalia. I overhead him saying sweetly to no one in particular, "Don't you want your stuff?" He was giving it all back.

However, the moment passed rather quickly. We had to be up early the next morning to take the train through the Chunnel into England for the last two shows and there was a ticketing problem when we got to the train station. A long line ensued and we were forced to sit tight until the problem was resolved. Piles of our luggage impeded the way for others. The situation was bordering on absurd as our group of weary travelers mostly ignored the plight of the French and English businessmen and women stumbling over and around our gear.

In the middle of this mess, one of the larger, louder members of the group began shouting across the station in a tone that clearly demonstrated his "ugly" Americanness. I was mortified by this breach in decorum. Across the queue, an attractive, middle-aged woman of undetermined nationality was observing the scene like a cultural anthropologist. She caught my eye as I shrank away in embarrassment from the crass behavior of one of our party. I immediately sensed her empathy. After the tumult had died down and the line began moving slowly but surely towards the customs checkpoint, she caught my eye again. Seemingly feeling and understanding everything that had transpired, she spoke to me in soothing French-accented English. She said, "Don't worry, we all love Americans now."

In keeping with their tradition of playing songs that fit the mood, the Radiators opened the first night's show at the Borderline in the Soho section of London with "Everybody Ought to Treat a Stranger Right, " which they segued into the O. V. Wright blues shakedown "Blind, Crippled and Crazy," with the great chorus, "I'd rather be blind, crippled and crazy, somewhere pushin' up daisies, than to let you break my heart all over again." They served up, "Searchin' for Soul," "Holiday" and teased, "Funky, Funky Broadway." The first encore, "My Home is on the Border" referenced the name of the club. The show concluded with an incendiary "Western Plains" followed by a reprise of "Treat A Stranger Right." The band was clearly on fire.

Though it was impossible to get to know everyone on the tour, a small group gathered the following afternoon, which was an off day and the first night of the tour without a show, at a local pub with the intent to crown royalty from among the fishheads. Over pints of Guinness, we were certain who would be our king. He was the only person who missed the bus to the train station in Paris. Yet by some quirk in European mass transit, he was waiting at the hotel in London with a cocktail in hand when the rest of the group arrived.

The last show of the tour was bittersweet. There were several snafus over the course of the trip that changed relationships; some for better, some for worse. But anyone who was expecting perfection was definitely deluded from the beginning—it was rock 'n' roll after all. They opened the set with "The Law of Fish" and the chorus of that song pretty much summed it up: "The big ones eat the little ones, the little got to be fast, 'cause that's the law of the fish, mama—you got to move your ass." The last song of the Radiators' European tour of 2001 was the Doors' "Soul Kitchen." "Well the clock says it's time to close now...."